'Jo Knight's heart beats strongly through this book: her heart for people, for planet and, most of all, for Jesus. With decades of global experience in relief, development, advocacy and creation care, Jo understands the scale and seriousness of the issues and weaves together voices of hope and challenge from diverse cultures with deep biblical insights. Her desire is to see the full scope of the gospel transforming communities and places with the good news of the Kingdom of God in all its fulness. I encourage you to read this book, to reflect on God's call and to act in response.'
Revd Dr Dave Bookless, Lausanne Global Catalyst for Creation Care, author of *Planetwise* and Head of Theology, A Rocha International

'Jo's passion and tireless advocacy for climate justice speaks through every page of *Called to Care.* Grounded in prophetic hope and resilience, she draws on Scripture, Pacific testimony and practical experience to offer churches a courageous roadmap from lament to transformative action. I endorse this timely book as essential reading for anyone seeking to embody Christ's love by safeguarding our Blue Pacific home, our global neighbourhood, and all creation.'
Revd James Bhagwan, General Secretary, Pacific Conference of Churches

'Full of biblical insight and practical stories, this book gives us hope. Hope that Christians can once again proclaim, "the earth is the Lord's". In a world where the scale of crisis can leave us feeling weary or uncertain, Jo Knight offers a gentle but prophetic invitation to respond – not with fear or fatalism, but with faith. Rooted in Scripture and rich in lived wisdom, this book reminds us that biblical hope is not passive. It empowers us to act, to pursue climate justice with courage, grace and love. A timely resource to help Christians reflect deeply and advocate boldly.'
Revd Tim Costello AO and Matt Darvas, Executive Directors, Micah Australia

I0807165

'It has been both a privilege and a joy to journey alongside Jo in our shared calling to creation care – planning and praying together, collaborating on campaigns and inviting the church to engage more deeply in this vital work. *Called to Care* is a beautiful expression of that journey. It reflects Jo's deep faith, her commitment to justice and her ability to listen to voices from around the world, including my own. This book will inspire you to reflect more deeply on your faith, and it will encourage you to act boldly and speak out with hope and conviction.'
Kuki (Lalbiakhlui) Rokhum, Director of Church Engagement, A Rocha International

'We live in a world with a deficit of hope. *Called to Care* offers a solid biblical foundation for a timely and much-needed response to one of the greatest challenges of our generation: *God works through His Holy Spirit and His Church – that's us!* With spiritual insight and practical wisdom, this book challenges Christians to rise up, take responsibility and become God's agents of change to heal His broken world.'
Tony Rinaudo AM, founder of Farmer Managed Natural Regeneration, agronomist, missionary and author

'My favourite Biblical text when confronted with the complex issues and challenges of climate justice is John 3:16. "For God so loved the world (Cosmos) that he gave his only Son…" From an Indigenous Christian perspective, this text articulates God's love for all His creation. As an Indigenous Christian climate justice advocate, I wholeheartedly commend Jo Knight's book. This timely work reminds us that addressing climate change is not only a moral imperative but a sacred calling – an act of love for God, for His creation, for each other and the generations yet to come. Rooted in Scripture and Spirit, this book powerfully calls the Church to embody justice, compassion and praxis for all His beloved creation.'
Pastor Uncle Ray Minniecon, Aboriginal Australian elder and advocate for First Nations' care for creation

'*Called to Care* is a powerful and much-needed invitation to the Church to reclaim its biblical calling to justice, stewardship and compassion in the face of climate breakdown. With theological depth, personal stories and practical tools for action, Jo Knight challenges Christians to embrace a holistic discipleship that cares for both people and planet. This is a timely and hope-filled resource for churches seeking to respond faithfully and boldly to the greatest moral challenge of our generation.'
Rudelmar Bueno de Faria, General Secretary, ACT Alliance

'In this compelling and uplifting book, Jo Knight invites us as her companions in a journey of call and response to the generational challenge of caring for God's creation. Sharing her faith insights and deep experience, Jo guides us to listen to God's call for holistic transformation in the world with its environmental crises, including through Scripture and spiritual reflection and through hope-filled testimonies from herself and other inspirational Christians. Jo then leads us to discern our own authentic response through prayerful and practical steps in an adventure of "spiritual rewilding": reimagining our own discipleship and the life-giving mission of the Church. This book is a precious and timely gift to nurture fresh hope and vital action.'
Revd Canon Rachel Carnegie, Chaplain at All Souls College, Oxford and past Executive Director of the Anglican Alliance

'*Called to Care* urges Christians to treat our world as if we really believe that God created it, and has gifted us life. Jo Knight shows why care for creation is not an add-on, or passing fad, but is grounded in Scripture and integral to our discipleship. Equally valuably, in this short and accessible book she provides practical pointers for how Christians of all traditions can act on the calling to care for people and planet, and through this plant the seeds of a revival in the life of the Church.'
Patrick Watt, CEO of Christian Aid

‘The barriers to solving the triple planetary crisis of climate change, biodiversity loss and pollution are not technical or scientific – we have all the tools we need to solve them. The barriers are spiritual – selfishness and apathy. Growing individualism and nationalism make Christians question whether we should care for our global neighbour and our common home. This challenging book, full of rich and accessible biblical wisdom and real lived out experiences of faith in action is timely and inspiring. It will help churches to tackle the spiritual crisis which underlies the climate one. This is our call – to faith filled action.’
Revd Canon Dr Rachel Mash, Coordinator of the Anglican Communion Environmental Network and leader of the Green Anglicans

‘Jo Knight has gifted the church with a compelling call to care for our creation. With both disarming gentleness and clear urgency, she presents a persuasive case for the church to take creation care seriously. This book combines biblical and theological reflection, prayerfulness and meditative suggestions, with accessible steps for individuals and churches to act and advocate. We Christians will do well to engage deeply with this book and respond to it wisely.’
Bishop Paul Barker, Anglican Diocese of Melbourne and Deputy Chair, Anglican Overseas Aid

‘*Called to Care* is a timely and inspiring book that connects the fight against poverty, inequality and climate change with stories of courage and practical action. It’s a moving reminder that lasting change comes when compassion and justice walk hand in hand.’
Simon Moss, Co-Founder of Global Citizen

‘We live in a world that is groaning – a world crying out under the weight of fractured relationships, neglected creation and lost connection with the divine. This cry is more than ecological crisis or societal unrest; it is the echo of our brokenness with God, with one another and with the earth that was entrusted to us as a gift. In *Called to Care*, Jo makes a critical call for faithful discipleship that demonstrates trust in the unwavering goodness of God while stepping courageously into the work of advocacy, reconciliation and healing.

Through the lens of Jo's insights drawn from diverse cultures and communities, we are reminded that even in the midst of deep suffering and disconnection, there is hope. For those who follow Jesus, the work of redemption is not distant or abstract – it is active, present, and deeply tied to how we care for both people and the planet.

This is a journey of rediscovery – of recognizing creation as God's good gift, and of reawakening to the truth that all life is interrelated, interdependent and sacred. The time to respond is now. The invitation is clear. Let us be a people who answer the call – not with fear, but with love, resolve and deep spiritual courage.'

Revd Melissa Lipsett, CEO of Baptist World Aid, Australia

To Peter, my rock, and our beautiful boys, Leo and Ezra.

CALLED TO CARE

A Christian response to the climate challenge of our generation

Jo Knight

ivp

First published in Great Britain in 2025

Inter-Varsity Press
Studio 101, The Record Hall, 16–16A Baldwin's Gardens, London EC1N 7RJ
https://ivpbooks.com

EU GPSR Authorised Representative
LOGOS EUROPE, 9 rue Nicolas Poussin, 17000, La Rochelle, France
Email: Contact@logoseurope.eu

British Library Cataloguing-in-Publication Data
A catalogue record for this book is available from the British Library

ISBN 978-1-7897-4505-4
eBook ISBN 978-1-7897-4506-1

10 9 8 7 6 5 4 3 2 1

Typeset by Fakenham Prepress Solutions, Fakenham, Norfolk NR21 8NL

First printed in Great Britain by Clays

eBook by Fakenham Prepress Solutions, Fakenham, Norfolk NR21 8NL

Produced on paper from sustainable sources

Inter-Varsity Press publishes Christian books that are true to the Bible and that communicate the gospel, develop discipleship and strengthen the church for its mission in the world.

IVP originated within the Inter-Varsity Fellowship, now the Universities and Colleges Christian Fellowship, a student movement connecting Christian Unions in universities and colleges throughout Great Britain, and a member movement of the International Fellowship of Evangelical Students. Website: www.uccf.org.uk. *That historic association is maintained, and all senior IVP staff and committee members subscribe to the UCCF Basis of Faith.*

FSC
www.fsc.org
MIX
Paper | Supporting responsible forestry
FSC® C018072

Contents

Acknowledgements

I acknowledge the Wurundjeri Woi-wurrung people of the Kulin Nation, the traditional custodians of the land where my story takes place, and pay my respect to their elders. I honour the unique role God has given Australia's first peoples and am grateful for the guidance of Aboriginal and Torres Strait Islander Christian leaders in my understanding of care for country and justice in God's big story.

I acknowledge my theological shaping in holistic mission and justice through many years of involvement in the Tearfund and integral mission movement, the Anglican Church globally, and the wisdom of Canon Dr Ruth Valerio and my husband, Revd Dr Peter Carolane. I am incredibly grateful for the interviewees who contributed specifically to this book: Canon Dr Ruth Valerio, Professor Katharine Hayhoe, Revd Dr Dave Bookless, Pastor Uncle Ray Minniecon, Ms Kuki Rokhum, Revd James Bhagwan, Pastor C. B. Samuel and Mr Tony Rinaudo AM. Thank you to my family, and to Christine Parrott, Daniel Nellor and Micah Wright-Taylor, for your reading and feedback; to my local church, Merri Creek Anglican, for the support of Anglican Overseas Aid; and to Tom Creedy and the IVP team for making this publication possible.

Foreword

As I sit here writing, my attention is caught by movement out of the corner of my eye. From where I sit, I look out of the kitchen window and onto the green that the post-second world war housing estate I live on has been built around. This is a fairly low area economically, but we have a high community spirit and have resisted attempts by the local authority to re-develop the area and build on the green. So in the middle of the estate is an attractive area with a football pitch, playground, lots of trees (many of which us residents have planted) and spaces that are unmown and full of wildflowers. As I look out the window, I can see a big tree. He is blowing in the wind and the movement of his branches, dancing this way and that, have caused me to look up from my laptop and watch.

I have lived here for thirty years and I realise I have been watching that tree grow for longer than I have been watching my daughters grow! I feel a strong sense of connection to this beautiful tree and were developers to try to cut him down I would do everything in my power to stop that happening, including with my body.

It is this sense of connection – of love – that Jo brings with her as she tackles this biggest issue of our time. The climate crisis is not about abstract ideas, political theories and scientific statistics (though all those things can play a part): the climate crisis is about love, for people and planet, for places and creatures, both near and far.

You will find in these pages three strands lovingly woven together. A deep appreciate of **Scripture** permeates through the book. Jo's desire to tackle the climate crisis and bring it to our attention comes from the heart of her Christian faith. **Stories** bring that desire to life as we hear about people from all over the world who, because of their faith, are taking action on the climate crisis. I am inspired and encouraged by the example of others, and I know you will learn from them too. Finally, Jo gives us very practical **Steps** so we can turn what we are reading about into well-thought-through action.

We face enormous challenges, but each one of us is called not to throw our hands up in despair and give in, but to stand together and act for and with this wonderful world that God has made. I know this book will help all of us do that more.

Canon Dr Ruth Valerio
Environmentalist and theologian, social activist and leader, public commentator and author of Saying Yes to Life

Introduction
What if we took God's call seriously?

Whether we live amid the dry savannah or the energy of urban life, we want the people and places we love to thrive for generations to come. We are facing a climate crisis that impacts the most vulnerable the hardest, threatening everything we hold dear. By coming together, we can work to protect our common home. As followers of Jesus, we are called to care for people and the natural world, and now is the time to take action. What if we fully embraced and integrated this calling into every aspect of our lives? Could our efforts lead to a transformative response to the defining challenge of our time?

This book presents stories, ideas and actions to encourage us to re-evaluate our purpose and embrace God's vision for the future. Addressing climate change is crucial because caring for God's creation is a profound expression of love for God, our neighbours and future generations. As new creations with God's Spirit within us, we are called to renew our minds and be inspired to undertake the good works that God has prepared for us. This is God's work in and through the Church.

Climate justice is about love in action. And who better to care and live out love than followers of Jesus? Our actions are love offerings that carry down the rushing streams and whisper on the wind to glorify our heavenly Father. Love beckons us to elevate the urgent transformations needed at every level of society for the sake of God's people and the planet, for everything we cherish. Climate justice prioritises those most affected, placing them at the forefront of our mission for survival.

The ideas and efforts that have inspired this book

I wrote this book because my work in international development and advocacy enables me to collaborate with people around the world as we tackle the challenges of poverty, climate change and injustice. Witnessing the global Church in action across diverse communities has been an incredible privilege. Two decades of advocating for global issues have taught me the importance of engaging with our world through both prayer and action, and I have come to appreciate the remarkable strength we possess when we unite as a Church.

I live in Melbourne, Australia, with my husband, Peter, an Anglican minister, and our two school-aged boys. I feel a deep compassion for our hurting and warming world, and I serve as the CEO of a non-profit organisation called Anglican Overseas Aid. I've always pursued a vocation that tries to make a difference in one way or another. This started with work as a lawyer representing refugees, and since then I've been involved in various efforts to combat poverty and climate change. I've advocated at international forums on behalf of the Church and have empowered countless everyday Christians to speak up for global justice to their elected leaders. These efforts go beyond my work and volunteering into my everyday living. I try to thoughtfully consider all aspects of life, from my family's weekly groceries to our values and practices, as we seek to live simply and fairly in our context.

I cherish the Church and am saddened that our response to pressing global issues often seems to lack vision, involvement and heartfelt action. Too often, we have become complacent in affluent societies, and now is the moment for us to awaken to our responsibility for the well-being of our world. In doing so, we will grow as disciples of Jesus.

You may be reading this book because you are concerned – either quietly or with alarm – about the impact of climate change, and you are seeking a faith-based response. It can be challenging to find like-minded Christians or discern how to move forward. Perhaps you yearn for the Church to broaden its focus to address the needs of the disadvantaged and the environmental crisis, in addition to personal salvation. When we fail to act in our world, we all suffer. Let's confront these challenges together.

How to read this book

One way to read this book is by working through a chapter each week during Lent and continuing *after* Easter, as our commitment to discipleship extends beyond a single season. The structure and design provide space to reflect and implement action. Whether paced for daily reading or longer periods, considered alone or with a group, may these pages help us navigate the challenges and joys of our Christian calling.

The book is divided into three parts, each framed with a 'call' and 'response':

- *Part 1* explores what the Bible says about our role in God's kingdom, justice and care for creation, and we will encounter a big gospel vision with implications for our discipleship and the Church's mission. We are reminded of our hope for God's world, where we allow God to inform our whole lives and, in doing so, stand up for the poor and for justice and care for creation. We rediscover and envisage what the Church can do, and learn from stories of the Church in action, leading with urgent hopefulness.
- *Part 2* connects us to the stories of people on the front lines of climate change. It calls out the problem and root causes in our Western systems and the silence or complicity of the Church in response. As we become more aware of the injustices and heartache, we turn to God in prayer and lament, address eco-anxiety and learn from global voices and perspectives.
- *Part 3* encourages us to contribute to hopeful change. It tells stories of individuals embracing their calling to care, providing models that we can follow. This section includes opportunities

for reflection on our own callings and action plans for the next steps. It explores how our individual actions, along with collective efforts, grow momentum and meaningful change as we strive for the beautiful tomorrow of God's renewed creation, free of poverty.

The book features summaries of interviews with a diverse group of practitioners, theologians and wise leaders who bring unique insights. I refer to them as contributors. They come from various backgrounds, with some focusing on environmental issues in high-consumer contexts, and others deeply rooted in traditional or Indigenous cultures:

- Katharine Hayhoe is an internationally acclaimed climate scientist and communicator, an academic and the author of *Saving Us*.
- Ruth Valerio is an environmentalist and theologian, a social activist and leader, a public commentator and author of *Saying Yes to Life*.
- James Bhagwan leads the Pacific Conference of Churches, championing ecological justice and responsibility.
- Dave Bookless is a theologian and conservationist, the author of *Planetwise* and a prominent figure leading global Church creation care.
- Ray Minniecon is an Aboriginal Australian elder, pastor and advocate for First Nations' care for creation.
- Kuki (Lalbiakhlui) Rokhum is an advocate in both the Indian and global Church; she is a leader in creation care and advocacy initiatives.
- C. B. Samuel is an Indian leader known for his work in integral mission and as an elder within the faith community.
- Tony Rinaudo is acclaimed as the founder of Farmer Managed Natural Regeneration, and an agronomist, missionary and author, contributing significantly to nature-based solutions.

Stories move us to action

As we read on, we will encounter heartfelt stories that inspire reflection and demonstrate what is possible. Our narratives hold the power to transform us; facts alone are not enough to drive action. I think that is why Jesus used stories so powerfully in his ministry. This is particularly true as we confront the climate crisis, where stories and connections are essential to activate shared values, moving and convicting us, and fostering hope.

Engaging with stories and models of holistic discipleship equips us to integrate these practices into our lives. Discipleship involves a commitment to following Jesus and actively engaging with the world through justice, advocacy and compassionate living;[1] it is a state reflected in how we live, not just what we believe.[2] Therefore, my hope is that this book will not simply be about gathering more information for you as a reader, but that it will inspire a change in your everyday practices.

This book offers space to discover your calling to care for the world, reminding us that our life experiences shape our choices and agency. Love motivates our actions, as expressed in 1 John 4:19: 'We love because he first loved us.' Our discipleship journey involves loving action and embracing counter-cultural values that promote maturity and simplicity in life. And as we do so, we become more like Jesus.

Integrating faith and climate justice

You might still be asking, 'What relevance does climate change have to my discipleship?' or, 'Isn't saving souls a higher priority?' But consider this: could we be missing something in God's plan and intention here on earth? What wisdom does God have for us regarding our role in loving his world, people and all in creation? Don't we want a faith that connects and makes sense of this and every challenge our world faces? What will we miss if we don't engage?

Jesus warns us of the consequences of inaction: 'For I was hungry and you gave me nothing to eat, I was thirsty and you gave me nothing to drink … Truly I tell you, whatever you did not do for one of the least of these, you did not do for me' (Matthew 25:42, 45b). What if someone's hunger or thirst was due to the climate crisis? What if the real 'least of these' in our time are those most affected by climate change?

There is often silence or even hostility within the Church regarding creation care and justice beyond simple charity. Many local churches downplay climate issues, viewing them as irrelevant or an aspect of partisan culture wars. Instead of addressing the root causes of the world's problems, we tend to focus on surface-level solutions. Environmental issues or structural justice and inequality have been overlooked in recent 'Western' Christian traditions and high-consumer contexts. Terms such as 'Western' or 'the Global North' are imperfect ways (which bear little resemblance to geography) to broadly refer to affluent contexts where people consume with relative abundance and they are used pragmatically in this book. It's important to recognise that inequality and diverse experiences of poverty also persist within these societies. Meanwhile, most people around the world experience life differently. They confront extreme poverty and growing inequality in environments where the natural resources are heavily burdened, struggling to provide the basics for survival. These tend to be lower- and middle-income nations representing around two-thirds of the world's population. This group is sometimes called the 'Majority World' or 'the Global South'.

Instead of avoiding these issues, let us draw strength from Jesus' words: 'Peace be with you! As the Father has sent me, I am sending you' (John 20:21). We are called to be agents of transformation and good. A growing movement in the Church is advocating for justice and creation care. However, we need to engage more people to respond to this call.

Our journey through these pages begins with biblical perspectives and ends with practical actions for addressing these challenges. We will discover that God's love for creation and justice for the poor is deeper than we might have realised. Our resurrected Jesus offers hope, and the Spirit empowers the Church to actively participate in God's renewal.

So, together, let's grapple with this question. It's a big one.

What if we took God's call to care for people and our planet seriously?

It's a question that takes us deep into our story with God.

It questions what we are saved for.

It invites us to unpack what we believe about God's plan for the future.

And it clarifies our role as God's image-bearers in our relationship with all in creation, inspiring us to play our part in God's kingdom of justice and flourishing.

Let's begin.

Part 1

1
Call: God's plan for all creation

This is what God the Lord says –
the Creator of the heavens, who stretches them out,
who spreads out the earth with all that springs from it,
who gives breath to its people,
and life to those who walk on it:
'I, the Lord, have called you in righteousness;
I will take hold of your hand.'
(Isaiah 42:5–6)

As Christians exploring climate justice, we must engage with what the whole Bible has to say about the whole of life, and in this case, the whole of creation. We should not just treat climate justice as a separate ethical or political stance. Fortunately, when it comes to this issue, God has a lot to say in the Scriptures. After all, he is the Creator 'who spreads out the earth with all that springs from it' (Isaiah 42:5).

Let's delve into the Bible's overarching theme of God, humanity and creation. I will utilise a helpful framework developed by theologian Ruth Valerio, who also contributed an interview for this book. This framework, which I refer to as 'God's big story in four parts', highlights how God relates to creation, the impact of sin on everything, how Jesus saves and transforms us, and how God will ultimately restore all things. Through this exploration, we will uncover God's heart and vision for the world and learn how we can align ourselves to these purposes. Ruth Valerio is a theologian and practitioner who has founded several initiatives that empower Christians to tackle poverty and environmental challenges. Her popular books inspire action based on biblical principles.

God's big story in four parts

First, God made this world, and God loves it. In Genesis 1:31, God looked at all God had made and said, 'It's very good.' We worship a God who thinks that this world is very good, and that in itself should say something to us. As people who worship and love God, don't we want to look after something which is so valuable to him? In Colossians 1:20, Paul says that Jesus' blood was shed on the cross to reconcile all things in heaven and on earth to God. So not only people but all things. God loves all things.
(Ruth Valerio)[1]

The book of Genesis is a theological statement about God, the creation and humanity. The American theologian Walter Brueggemann describes Genesis as a 'faith statement'.[2] Two such faith statements covered in Genesis 1 are: God created the creation, and God thought his creation was good.

What does the writer of Genesis mean by 'good'? English translations of the Hebrew sometimes write 'good' and other times write 'beautiful' – the original Hebrew word has enough flexibility in its meaning to go either way. One way it is good and beautiful is that the creation exists in harmony, and time and space, light and darkness, flora and fauna all work together in a perfect ecosystem to form an Edenic paradise. This harmony significantly encompasses God, people and the creation as a whole, indicated by how God 'blessed' it (Genesis 1:22, 28). All creatures (animals and humans alike) had perfect relationships with one another and their Creator. All we need to do to encounter its beauty is stand at the bottom of a free-flowing waterfall or under the lush branches of an old tree, hear the sounds of birds calling in the morning or swim in the ocean.

If we take this seriously, then we will take climate justice seriously. If we believe that God lovingly created a good and beautiful world, why would we not want to care for that world? Perhaps we are thinking dualistically – dividing the physical and spiritual worlds. But a Christianity infected by dualism leads to the wrong thinking that God is interested only in the spiritual realm. If that were the case, then it would be easy to conclude that God provided the earth for us to simply exploit, and it would also make us suspicious of science, as we will explore below.

Like an artist, God speaks through his good and beautiful creation. John Stott made this vital point in his chapter on Charles Darwin in his book *People My Teachers*:

> It is an intriguing concept that God has written not one book, but two. The book of God's Word we call 'Scripture', and the book of God's Works 'Nature'. Both are divine revelations, the disclosure of God's glory in nature and of his grace in Scripture. Moreover, he invites us to study both, so that nature study and Bible study should go hand in hand. And as we engage in these studies we find ourselves, in the famous words of the German astronomer Johannes Kepler, 'thinking God's thoughts after him'.
>
> In consequence, there is an important correspondence between theology and science. Theology is the human attempt to understand and synthesize what God has revealed in Scripture, while science is the human attempt to understand and systematize what God has revealed in nature.[3]

The Bible is full of examples of God using the creation to speak to people. Think of the Old Testament prophets and Jesus, who went up the mountains to draw closer to God. Jesus used animals and birds to communicate God's word. Birds teach us about faith subjects such as repentance, self-esteem, gratitude, work, freedom, joy and love.[4] As Stott repeatedly argued, 'nature study and Bible study should go together'.[5] Jeremiah, for example, uses the migration flight patterns of storks to talk about repentance (Jeremiah 8:7), and Jesus talks about the feeding of ravens to explain faith (Luke 12:24). In the Sermon on the Mount, Jesus famously told his audience in Matthew 6:26–28 to look at the birds of the air and see how the flowers of the field grew. Even Martin Luther observed, 'You see, he is making the birds our schoolmasters and teachers ... Whenever you listen to a nightingale, therefore, you are listening to an excellent preacher.'[6]

God also speaks through trees. I'm forever bringing my family under the canopy of incredible trees to gaze up to great heights. Isaiah 41:19–20 describes the hope of Israel in a full and lush forest with a variety of species of trees. Mountains, rains, birds or trees all point to God as the provider and sustainer of all things. God's creation is undoubtedly good and beautiful.

This section has introduced the first principle of climate justice theology: God created a good and beautiful world, and therefore we should love what the Creator loves. Our God is a divine artist who reveals truth to us through all creation. As a result, we should not view creation as a commodity; instead, we should recognise it as inherently good and a reflection of God's wisdom.

God's gardeners

The second part of God's big story is our role as God's representatives in the world, ruling creation with love as its gardeners.

> **Second, we've been created and placed in this world to take care of the rest of what God has made.** We have been created to be God's representatives in the wider world; we've been created in God's image so that we might rule over the birds of the air and the fish of the sea and so on. We must remember God's idea of ruling is never about oppression or tyranny but, in God's eyes, is always about love and compassion, thinking of the other and ultimately servanthood. We've been created as God's servant rulers to take care of the rest of what he's made.
> (Ruth Valerio)[7]

Genesis makes it clear that the earth, the plants and creatures, and even the sun and moon are God's creations and, therefore, not divine in themselves. This is important because it enables people to confidently interact with creation without fearing it is something to be worshipped. In fact, God commands Adam to care for the garden (Genesis 2:15), which sets a pattern for us to care for creation. This is part of what it means when the creation story makes the faith statements that people are made in God's image and have 'dominion' over the creation. We are called to be good gardeners – good 'rulers' of the creation (Genesis 1:28–30). This means treating the earth and everything in it in a way that brings glory to God. It means living as God intended.

We must not abuse our God-given responsibility. God expects people to exercise their authority over the creation righteously. We have a moral calling and obligation to the creation in a way the other animals do not. Since our authority to rule over creation comes from God, the pattern of that rule must also come from God.

As we exercise our authority over creation, it is essential that we embody God's character of justice. This means our stewardship should reflect God's attributes of love, grace, holiness, justice and truth, ensuring that our actions align with God's just nature as depicted in the Scriptures. We worship a God of justice, and everything God does is just (Genesis 18:25; Deuteronomy 32:4). Isaiah noted that God's justice would be a light to the nations (Isaiah 51:4). Jeremiah stated that the Lord delights in kindness, justice and righteousness (Jeremiah 9:24). Psalm 36:6 expresses God's care for all creatures, while Ezekiel portrays God as a shepherd healing the injured (Ezekiel 34:16). The book of Job teaches that true wisdom involves trusting in God's perfect justice, even when it is hard to understand. The God of the Bible is just, and understanding that true worship means seeking justice and caring for the poor and vulnerable encourages us to fulfil our calling to live justly.

Also, we must remember that we are living things, too – we are part of creation. Climate scientist Katharine Hayhoe reminds us,

> Scientifically, we are very much part of creation because 50% of the oxygen we breathe comes from microscopic phytoplankton in the ocean. So we can't survive without

> nature, as we can't float around in outer space without nature. It doesn't need us. The planet, plants and animals would be fine without us, but we need them.[8]

We should, therefore, balance our identity as rulers over creation with the reality that, in the words of Isaiah 40:6b–8,

> All people are like grass,
> and all their faithfulness is like the flowers of the field.
> The grass withers and the flowers fall,
> because the breath of the Lord blows on them.
> Surely the people are grass.
> The grass withers and the flowers fall,
> but the word of our God endures for ever.

We are set apart from creation, but not all that far apart. Our existence is as fragile as that of any other creature or plant. We exist interdependently with creation. What we do to the natural world impacts other creatures as well as humans. For example, the absence of trees and healthy seas reduces our world's capacity to process carbon dioxide, and the overall climate heats up. Similarly, if certain species of animals become extinct, this disrupts the balance of the whole ecosystem.

As theologian Dave Bookless reminds us, there are two opposite truths we can forget as we consider our responsibility over creation.[9] On the one hand, we can forget that we are made in God's image and downplay the uniqueness of human beings in the creation. Then, we would be no different from any other animal on the planet. The other truth we can forget is that we are made from 'dust' (Genesis 2:7) and are very much part of the creation. Balancing these two truths enables us to be the righteous gardeners God calls us to be, and we will experience the freedom and joy of people who align with God's purposes.[10]

In the first of the four parts of God's overarching story, we learned that God's creation is good and beautiful. In this section, we have expanded on that idea to explore what it means to be made in God's image and how we can relate to creation as God intended, as good gardeners. God is just and seeks that we rule over creation righteously and remember that we, too, are created.

The creation is frustrated because of sin

The third part of God's big story addresses the impact of sin on creation and our responsibility to collaborate with God in healing our world's brokenness.

> **Third, this world has gone wrong because of us.** That's pretty obvious, and the Bible reflects that too. There are biblical passages in the Prophets that talk about how people's sin has a connection to the land that mourns or revolts. For example, Jeremiah 4, or Hosea 8, reveals that when we don't worship God and are not taking care of other people, the land responds negatively. So the world has gone wrong because of us. We, therefore, have a responsibility to put it back to right. But we don't do that in our own strength.
> (Ruth Valerio)[11]

While God expected us to rule over creation righteously, Genesis 3 tells the tragic story of how humanity did not resist the temptations of selfish rule. The perfect harmony between God, humanity and the land, as discussed in part 1 of Ruth's framework, turned to dissonance when Adam and Eve sinned and God imposed judgement (Genesis 3:14–19). Sin revealed a fractured image needing restoration, and this extended to our stewardship of the creation.

We see this brokenness play out in the climate crisis. The pursuit of wealth and extraction from the earth, no matter the cost, overtakes our relationship with God and unjustly harms relationships with our fellow human beings and our natural world. Governments and corporations choose profits over justice: insatiable growth over sustainability.

The relationship between people became fractured, and their relationship with God shifted from the innocence of their nakedness to the shame and hiddenness behind fig leaves (Genesis 3:7). This was when God appeared in person, entered the garden 'in the cool of the day' (Genesis 3:8) and spoke directly to the people, asking them to give an account of their actions and then pronouncing judgement.[12] As we reflect on the disruption of harmony, consider how climate change negatively impacts people's lives. For instance, a coastal community that depends on fishing for its livelihood now struggles due to the destruction of coral reefs and declining fish populations caused by industrial pollution and rising sea temperatures. Human activity has harmed the environment, disrupted the ecosystem and made it increasingly difficult for the community to catch fish. This situation results in food insecurity and economic hardship for families.

God's judgement included a curse on creation. The blessing of God's abundant supply of food (Genesis 1:29–30) and the joy of the good and rewarding work of caring for the garden turned into the curse of the trials of hard and often fruitless work, and the newly introduced 'thorns and thistles' (Genesis 3:18; 4:12). People work hard all their lives, and they lie awake all night stressing about it, and then they die. It leads to nothing: 'This too is meaningless' (Ecclesiastes 2:22–23). This is all a description of the terrible way the creation is 'subjected to futility' and the 'bondage to decay' (Romans 8:20–21, NRSVA) because of sin. God had originally spoken the creation into existence with a good purpose, but that purpose became impossible to reach.

Anyone living on the planet knows that the creation is frustrated. Every time we hear of a terrible famine or another animal that is on the endangered list, the futility is playing itself out. There has been a breakdown in the relationship between people and God, which has consequences for the relationship between people and creation. We see this in the Old Testament with Israel's relationship to the land. Israel experiences blessings and curses with regard to the land, depending on the choices they make towards or away from God – and this remains true for all of us.[13] Such connectedness between our actions and the land is powerfully expressed in the final passage of Job's words in Job 31:38–40:

If my land cries out against me
and all its furrows are wet with tears,
if I have devoured its yield without payment
or broken the spirit of its tenants,
then let briers come up instead of wheat
and stinkweed instead of barley.

The frustration of the creation does not mean that, at the same time, we cannot experience beauty and wonder in creation. As we considered in part 1 of our framework, 'God's invisible qualities – his eternal power and divine nature' are on display so that nobody has any excuse not to know the truth (Romans 1:20). Paul goes on to explain this tension between beauty and frustration by describing it as like a heavily pregnant woman 'groaning' in the pains of childbirth (Romans 8:22), longing in hope for its future renewal.

Another consequence of the fracture in relationships is poverty and inequality. Injustice towards the vulnerable is deeply abhorrent to God. The law of Moses, particularly the laws in Leviticus – including the principle of Jubilee – demonstrates that God values just societies and cares for the poor and foreigners. Isaiah emphasises that God is exalted by justice and shows his holiness through it. The prophets Amos and Micah call attention to God's love for the poor and the pursuit of justice, which is true worship: 'do justice, ... love kindness, and ... walk humbly with your God' (Micah 6:8, NRSVA).

God's justice encompasses both judgement and mercy (Deuteronomy 10:17–18) and brings great joy (Psalm 19:8; 67:4; 98:9). On an appointed day, Jesus will judge the world with justice (Acts 17:31), revealing his righteous acts and prompting all nations to worship (Revelation 15:3–4). Latin American theologian Ruth Padilla DeBorst explains that justice is God's redemptive restoration of what is wrong. She continues, 'Justice sets things right; it vindicates the victims of climate disaster and human oppression.'[14] God desires his justice to be reflected in his people and he loves those who show mercy (Jeremiah 22:3; Micah

6:8). However, he judges those who commit injustice (Isaiah 5:1–7).

After warning Israel of impending judgement for their injustices, Isaiah foretold the coming of a Suffering Servant: 'In faithfulness he will bring forth justice' (Isaiah 42:3). Jesus fulfils this role, demonstrating God's perfect justice by dying on the cross for the sins of the world (Romans 3:25–26).

Jesus comes to redeem and renew

The wonderful fourth part of God's story is that Jesus comes to renew our world.

> **Fourth, the good news is that God has a plan for his whole creation.** We see this in passages like Colossians 1, Romans 8 and Revelation 21 and 22. The Bible doesn't speak about the world being destroyed and us spending the rest of our days in a different place. Instead, the world the Bible speaks about as 'new' is in terms of renewal, that the heavens and the earth will be renewed and transformed. And so God has a future for this world. And we are called to be a part of that and to live our lives in a way that looks forward to and anticipates that future.
> (Ruth Valerio)[15]

For Christians who are concerned about climate justice, our great hope is the promise that, at the end of time, God will finally free creation from its frustration (Romans 8:19–23).[16] In fact, Jesus has a special role in ruling supreme over this process of new creation:

> The Son is the image of the invisible God, the firstborn over all creation. For in him all things were created: things in heaven and on earth, visible and invisible, whether thrones or powers or rulers or authorities; all things have been created through him and for him. He is before all things, and in him all things hold together. And he is the head of the body, the church; he is the beginning and the firstborn from among

> the dead, so that in everything he might have the supremacy. For God was pleased to have all his fullness dwell in him, and through him to reconcile to himself all things, whether things on earth or things in heaven, by making peace through his blood, shed on the cross.
> (Colossians 1:15–20)

Take time to read slowly and consider the depths and implications of that passage. The Son of God rules supreme over the first creation, and because of this, he rules supreme over the new creation. Paul rejoices that the Son of God brings reconciliation and peace through his perfect sacrifice (Colossians 1:20). This peace exists between people and God, people and people, and people and creation.[17] God's mission is not limited to saving humanity alone. Notice the ripple effect of cosmic healing which begins in Christ's resurrected body, extends out to all those who are in Christ, 'the firstfruits of the Spirit' (Romans 8:23), and finally applies to the rest of the universe in the second creation – the New Heaven and Earth.[18]

This Colossians passage inspires us to embrace a bigger vision of the gospel and God's struggle for the good of creation here on earth. It invites us to acknowledge that Christ's reconciliation through the cross encompasses 'all things' on 'earth'. Let us revalue the significance of our planet and align with the intentions of our Creator God.

As we have worked through Ruth Valerio's biblical framework of God's big story, we have delved into the creation story, the profound beauty of God's work and the promise of redemption and renewal in Christ. We are tasked with becoming stewards of the earth, tending it as God's gardeners, recognising the damage we've caused, while seeking to play a part in healing it.

Implication: the meaning of heaven

What we think about the end of time, 'eschatology', shapes our behaviour in the present. Revelation 21 – 22 offers a vision of the new creation, a place where God lives among his people (21:3) and where there will be no more sadness or pain (21:4). While the first creation was a garden, the second creation will be a Holy City, the New Jerusalem, coming down to earth (21:2). At the centre of this city will be a garden containing the tree of life, the Son of God, providing eternal life for the children of God (22:2).

This side of Christ's second coming, we may not fully understand what this means, but the clues suggest that the New Heaven and Earth will be something like a renewed Eden – similar to yet distinct from the first paradise with both continuity and change. This mirrors the transformation seen in Jesus' body after the resurrection, as he was strangely both recognisable and mysteriously different (Matthew 28:1–10; Mark 16:1–8; Luke 24:13–49; John 20).

Dave Bookless was taught as a child that he would go to heaven after death while waiting for Jesus to judge the world. In that church tradition, the assumption was that the earth will be destroyed in the 'fire' of God's judgement (2 Peter 3:10) because that was the prevailing language from the King James Bible translation. With this framing, there's little need to care for our world. Perhaps this has been your assumption, too? Later, Dave understood that the Bible affirms God's plan to renew creation. Using the most recent biblical scholarship on 2 Peter 3:10, he came to a more accurate translation: 'that the world and all that is in it will be discovered and revealed. It's almost like the picture of a forest fire; when the fire has come through, the green shoots come up.'[19]

In his writing, particularly in *Planetwise*, Dave Bookless explores what the Bible says about creation and the New Heaven and New Earth. He highlights the story of Noah, where, after the flood, creation was renewed, not replaced, evident in God's covenant symbolised by a rainbow.[20] He emphasises concepts such as renewal and restoration and perhaps even recycling.[21] Jesus' death and resurrection repair our broken relationships, and this offers hope for a future where Jesus restores, rather than destroys, our physical world.

Another assumption that can limit our care for the earth is the belief that we will ascend to heaven. I had the opportunity to participate in a conversation with scholar N. T. Wright, who explained that in the biblical story, 'the whole point is God coming to dwell in and with his creation'.[22] God's vision is for the renewal of all things, on earth as it is in heaven. He urged Christians to shift away from the idea of humans ascending to heaven, highlighting that the Bible is about God creating a world to inhabit with us. Wright explained that when we have a clearer understanding of how God comes to earth and ultimately is joined, the relationship between the Old Testament and the New Testament becomes much clearer, and so does the task of the Church.[23] He pointed out that the Church has neglected its responsibility to care for creation, and that Christians must articulate their duty in the struggle for God's good creation.[24] Indeed, while parts of the Church have often overlooked the importance of creation care, there is a growing movement that recognises the integration of our relationship with Christ and how we act in relation to the earth,[25] articulated significantly by the Lausanne Cape Town Commitment.[26]

We have explored God's plan for all creation and the overarching vision of the gospel. This reminds us of our hope for God's world and implications for our discipleship and the mission of the Church. Next, we will explore God's desire for his people to live justly and restore what is broken.

Implication: the meaning of salvation

This book opened with a question: What if we took God's call to care for people and our planet seriously? Are we saved to play a part in caring for God's world? Yes! We are saved because we are loved by God, created to participate in his good purposes. When Jesus launched his kingdom mission in Nazareth in Luke 4:16–21, he revealed that God's kingdom and good purposes extend beyond expectations. Jesus read carefully and selectively from Isaiah and highlighted his particular concern for people experiencing poverty and marginalisation:

> The Spirit of the Lord is on me,
> because he has anointed me
> to proclaim good news to the poor.
> (Luke 4:18)

He also referred to the concept of Jubilee from Leviticus 25, announcing freedom for prisoners and a reset for creation. After reading, Jesus declared, 'Today this scripture is fulfilled in your hearing' (Luke 4:21).

This passage reminds us that Jesus is active in our world *today*. And it is *now* that God's kingdom on earth is taking shape. Now, he works through his Holy Spirit and his Church. That's us! And we are saved to play a part in this great story. Jesus invites us into his upside-down kingdom with its far-reaching implications. This is a great kingdom where his people live upside down to many of the values around them, practise radical generosity and serve people experiencing poverty. It is a kingdom where his people practise release and reset in care for all creation. And this extends to every aspect of our lives – from how we live, consume, vote and pray. When facing the world's brokenness, we find hope in Jesus and accept the call to contribute to healing and restoration, recognising that we are not alone in this mission. We hold the tension of not simply waiting idly for change, nor trying to fix everything in our own strength. God is sovereign, and we are saved to play a part in his good purposes on earth.

Implication: the meaning of justice

Living justly reflects our humanity as intended by God. As we act as God's good 'gardeners', tilling the earth and bringing physical order, so too do we bring moral order by promoting justice and embodying peace. Ruth Padilla DeBorst explains, 'The fruit of justice is *shalom*, peace, the flourishing of life, and the realization of God's good purposes.'[27] Grace inspires us to pursue justice as disciples of Jesus. As Tim Keller noted, true understanding of God's grace leads to just actions. If someone claims to appreciate this grace but neglects the poor, it indicates a lack of understanding of God's mercy.[28]

We are called to address injustice, and true worship involves action, not just words. Indian church leader C. B. Samuel urges, 'The Bible expects those who wish for the Kingdom to be located among those who feel the pain of the Kingdom being violated.'[29] Pacific church leader James Bhagwan makes the similar point that 'you cannot do theology with your backs to the suffering of people'.[30] We follow Jesus, the man of sorrows familiar with suffering (Isaiah 53:3), who shared life and ministry with those who were poor and marginalised. Indeed, the early church grasped this as they encouraged Paul's ministry: 'They asked only one thing, that we remember the poor, which was actually what I was eager to do' (Galatians 2:10, NRSVA). We, too, must remember the poor, following the model of the early church, and pursue justice and compassion.

Tackling poverty and the breakdown of our natural world requires us to address root causes, not just alleviate suffering. Ruth Padilla DeBorst challenges those of us in the Global North to embrace our biblical calling, respond with sacrifice to the cry of the people and the earth, and recognise our complicity in the very systems that perpetuate injustice.[31] She encourages us to reject our idols of success and consumerism, and reflect on how our churches can function as prophetic communities against these influences.[32]

As we acknowledge our calling to participate in God's good purposes, we start to grasp what it truly means to live justly and address the challenges in our world. At times, our limited imagination of what is possible can hold us back, so it is important to embrace a hopeful vision for God's people that exceeds our expectations.

Reflection

We have reached our first moment for reflection.

Take time to pause. It is designed to encourage contemplation and provide some breathing space to reflect on the words and ideas.

At the end of each reflection, there is a prayer.

What new connections might God be inviting you to make today?

How have you experienced a glimpse of God's revelations in nature's beauty?

Step outside – whether to a local creek, park or beach – and take a moment to be still.

Engage your senses and appreciate God's wisdom in all of creation.

Be still and know that God's declaration is 'very good'.
Rest under his loving gaze.
Nature proclaims the glory of the Creator.
Just be present and enjoy the moment.

I've been resting with God, practising this exercise with the weight of ancient rocks and Aboriginal cave paintings hanging over me at Gariwerd Grampians National Park in Victoria, Australia. I sat in the winter sun with a cool breeze, finishing a sandwich. I absorbed far-ranging views, locking them in my mind before my return to the concrete of my city life. I stilled my soul. I noticed the ants that were busy shifting my breadcrumbs. There is no waste in God's creation; the ants were part of that order. The red rock felt nearly smooth to me but presented as valleys and mountains to the hardworking ants. Creator God is incredible, the Ancient of Days in these lands – now and always. I began to pray: God, you declare these lands 'very good'. You declare these ants 'very good'. You declare my family, wandering across these rocks, 'very good'. Thank you, God.

Now it's your turn.

What do you discern as you sit with God in creation?

Conclude with this prayer:

Loving God,
Thank you for this time in your creation.
Help me to be a good gardener, tending to the world with love and respect.
May I honour all that you have made and nurture it with care.
Amen.

2
Response: holistic transformation

> The kingdom of heaven is like a mustard seed, which a man took and planted in his field. Though it is the smallest of all seeds, yet when it grows, it is the largest of garden plants and becomes a tree, so that the birds come and perch in its branches.
> (Matthew 13:31–32)

You may have noticed that the chapters of this book alternate between a 'call' and a 'response'. In the first chapter, we reflected on God's plan for all of creation and the overarching vision of the gospel. We examined the biblical call to care for the earth as God's gardeners, acknowledging the harm we have caused and our responsibility in healing it. We were reminded of our hope for God's world and the implications this has for our discipleship and the mission of the Church to live justly and tackle the challenges we face in today's world. In this chapter, we will consider our response, which is 'mission'.

Let me introduce a concept that may or may not be new to you: 'holistic transformation'. This involves bringing the good news of the gospel to the world in word and deed. It is also known as 'holistic mission' or 'integral mission'. It responds to the idea that we don't ignore the world because that would betray God's sending us out to serve the world, and nor do we ignore the biblical call and have nothing to bring to the world. Instead, justice, political action and structural change in our physical world belong together with spiritual, personal change and worship. 'As in the life of Jesus, being, doing and saying are at the heart of our integral task.'[1] Mission can be challenging to think about when we live in a time when the Church in the West seems to be in rapid retreat. Most churches in the West are in survival mode and are not fulfilling their social nor their evangelistic responsibility, with limited engagement in acts of justice or care for the natural world (we'll explore this more in part 2 of the book). But we can have hope. What we will see in this chapter is that holistic mission leads to spiritual renewal in our churches. In God's good design, holistic mission is actually good for the Church and good for the world. As we learned in chapter 1, God has made us in his image to be his caretakers of the world – and when we live this out, the world flourishes.

As we strive to be beacons of justice, healing and reconciliation for all creation, we have the opportunity to rediscover the Church's potential. We are part of a living network of believers who share the same source of life and love. God nurtures us and places others around us so that we can grow in vibrancy and diversity. In his wisdom, this design is beneficial for us and for the world he loves. In our time, the Church can experience renewal and foster flourishing life. As believers shaped by God's transforming power, we are invited to act with urgent hope for the sake of all creation. As we discern how to live this out, we may need to reimagine what the Church could look like and draw inspiration from examples of faithful individuals who go before us.

My husband, Peter, has been inspiring our local church with a vision of rewilding the Church in our secular inner-city community. He was particularly moved by a lesson from nature in the breathtaking Scottish Highlands, where the barren hills were once covered with lush forests teeming with wildlife. He read an article in *The Scotsman* that said, 'Scotland's natural beauty is both a source of national pride and a seductive draw for tourists across the globe; it would surprise most to learn that it ranks among the most nature-depleted countries in the world.'[2] This made him wonder how people could accept such a depleted landscape as normal. He saw the Scottish Highlands as a metaphor for the state of Christianity in Western culture. Might we, too, need to reimagine what the Church could be, much like the hopeful idea of rewilding?

We often become accustomed to our surroundings, even if they are not ideal. There was a time when Christianity flourished in the West, but since the Second World War it has declined, and Church attendance has plummeted. We still see some of the echoes of Christianity influencing the culture, but Christianity is being marginalised and muted, becoming like a dry and desolate land. Mark Sayers writes in his book *Disappearing Church* that many people want the kingdom without the King in post-Christian culture.[3] You may live in a neighbourhood like mine, where there are some signs of spiritual life, but it feels like a spiritual wasteland for the most part. Many churches in my local community are empty, sold off, demolished or rapidly declining. Christianity is being pushed to the edges or seen as irrelevant.

Now is the time for the Church, especially in the West, to reimagine its life-giving mission and be open to new approaches. This shift should lead to a more holistic engagement with our world. When we practise whole-of-life discipleship as followers of Jesus, our local churches can demonstrate truly transformative and life-giving change. As God declared in the book of Amos,

> Away with the noise of your songs!
> I will not listen to the music of your harps.
> But let justice roll on like a river,
> righteousness like a never-failing stream!
> (Amos 5:23–24)

Putting into practice the pursuit of justice and caring for creation are essential components of life in the kingdom.

There is hope. We can reimagine and rewild our churches to be life-giving and inspiring agents of change. Similar to the passionate movement aimed at restoring ecological life to Scotland's Highlands, which balances human intervention with allowing nature to take its course, we can learn from these examples to envision our churches as balancing planning with spontaneity, and structure with freedom. This approach can enhance how the Church shapes individuals, shares the word and engages in social action. Just as Jesus likened spreading the gospel to a farmer sowing seeds (Luke 8:5–15), we can envision the potential of rewilding to bring ecological life to the land, paralleling the potential of holistic ministry to bring kingdom life to our neighbourhoods.

Holistic role modelling

As we reimagine what the Church could look like, as in the metaphor of spiritual rewilding, let's turn to people who are modelling this practically.

C. B. Samuel's story

C. B. Samuel, an Indian Christian leader, is a compassionate friend to the poor in his country. His teachings also shape those who are wealthy, providing profound observations and insights that enhance their discipleship. C. B. Samuel is a mild-mannered giant of holistic mission and biblical teaching in the global Church. He is always neatly dressed in a collarless kurta, with glasses and a clipped white beard. C. B. is passionate about role-modelling discipleship and the Church as an agent of transformation in our world.

He reminds us that those who encountered Jesus in the Gospels embraced his character and concern for the 'least of these' (Matthew 25:40). Zacchaeus, a repentant tax collector, realised he needed to repay those he had exploited (Luke 19:8). C. B. Samuel notes that the early church actively engaged with the marginalised. He cites Mother Teresa as a modern example of radical service and compassion for the poor in India, and notes that many of her volunteers were inspired to change their lifestyles as well. However, C. B. Samuel observes that this holistic approach has been lacking across the modern Church, with insufficient teaching and modelling.[4]

The holistic transformation movement emerged as a response to this situation, affirming that evangelism and social action are inseparable aspects of the Church's mission and gospel demonstration. Also known as integral mission, this movement views 'mission' as the transformation of society, encompassing holistic development of individuals and communities.[5] Leaders from the Global South, such as René Padilla (who coined the term *misión integral* or 'integral mission')[6] and many others, including C. B. Samuel, played significant roles through the Lausanne and Micah networks.[7]

C. B. Samuel encourages the Church to embrace holistic transformation that incorporates both emotional and spiritual dimensions, rather than limiting its mission to isolated activities such as evangelism, social action or creation care. Drawing from his experience leading the development organisation EFICOR (The Evangelical Fellowship of India Commission on Relief) and mentoring individuals, he emphasises that the Church should focus on shaping people, sharing the word and engaging in social action. By combining these elements, the Church can achieve true transformation. I am grateful that, as a young adult learning under C. B. in India, my faith was shaped in this holistic way. C. B. warns that many people in Western-thinking contexts leave local churches for parachurch organisations because they do not find the churches to be places of transformation. He laments that many organisations focus solely on development or evangelism, with local churches merely providing financial support. 'By excluding the Church, we lose the essential ability to transform society,' he states.[8] The Church should not be seen as just another organisation; it is a living entity, like a vine with its branches, as described by Jesus in John 15. This imagery encourages us to rethink the shape and focus of the Church.

James Bhagwan and the Pacific Church: prophetic, practical and pastoral

On his paddle-board, Reverend James Bhagwan feels a deep connection to the ocean surrounding his island home in Fiji. He marvels at the beauty and diversity of God's creation and feels a responsibility to protect it. His time is precious, as he leads the Pacific Conference of Churches in a challenging and demanding ecumenical role. James travels the world to represent the voices of the Pacific; he speaks to the public and media about the urgent issues facing his region. He cares for the people who are losing their homes and livelihoods to the rising seas, and he balances this with his duties as a husband and a father. James is driven by his passion for the Pacific and his commitment to do everything he can to save island life.[9]

James's early ministry brought him to a parish serving marginalised communities squatting precariously on reclaimed parts of mangroves in shacks made out of roofing and timber wrecked by cyclones. At a similar time, James served as a chaplain to Fiji's traditional voyaging society and he grasped the importance of the sea. He explains,

> The ocean is the second lung of the planet, the blue lung. I always say that for every two breaths we take, one is from the trees, and one is from the seas. Recognising the health and vulnerability of the ocean is so important because of climate change and plastic pollution.[10]

From there, God grew James to be a prophetic voice and leader across the denominations of Oceania, standing up in subsequent years for the Pacific peoples and the natural world.

The Church in the Pacific models an integrated response to the climate crisis, from helping people relocate to higher ground as sea levels rise, to lobbying at international climate negotiations. The Pacific churches have a threefold approach to their work: prophetic, pastoral and practical. They are responding to God's call in holistic ways to transform society.

James Bhagwan explains that prophetic Pacific voices sparked the World Council of Churches' first significant statement on climate change more than two decades ago, urging the more developed and polluting countries and their churches to take action and reduce their carbon emissions.[11] At that time, the Pacific churches were addressing theological misconceptions among their people, as they thought God's promise to Noah meant that their islands would never flood. The church leaders helped people understand the human causes of climate change and the scientific evidence. James continues to speak out about non-economic loss, damage and the implications of climate relocation, while calling for the phase-out of fossil fuels.

Pacific Church pastoral care builds people's capacity and resilience. When forced to relocate from island homes, very vulnerable people look for practical and spiritual support. On a practical front, the Pacific churches have been rebuilding places of worship after disasters and serving as community and evacuation centres.[12]

There is much to learn from the models of Christian sisters and brothers in holistic, transformative responses to the world around us. Consider how you could encourage transformation, like spiritual rewilding, in your own context. How might you welcome different perspectives, expressions and gifts to nurture a holistic mission? As with nature, rewilding takes time. Trust that God is at work cultivating patience and faith, even when you cannot see immediate results.

Christians shaping a brighter future for our planet

> And let us consider how we may spur one another on towards love and good deeds.
> (Hebrews 10:24)

This next section presents a variety of examples of holistic transformation and illustrates how God is actively renewing and fostering these responses. Diverse leaders from around the world are implementing holistic approaches to mission, aiming to create positive change for our planet. The stories include my experiences with a growing movement among God's people, individual accounts of combining faith with advocacy, local churches engaging with their communities, and the efforts of the Church at global denominational levels.

The key takeaway is that there are numerous ways to envision our response to God's holistic call for transformation as the Church. In part 3, we will consider additional examples of individuals discovering God's call and formulating responses. Sharing ideas is an excellent way to inspire one another towards love and good deeds (Hebrews 10:24). May these examples motivate us to find new ways to engage as the Church with the world.

In my interview with Katharine Hayhoe, we discussed many ways in which followers of Jesus holistically respond to God's call and shape a hopeful future. Some may run soup kitchens, or raise charitable funds, while others focus on advocacy. There is no single way to fulfil God's purpose; whatever we do should be characterised by love. Katharine notes, 'It will be very clear that it's motivated by love, and it's expressing love, and it's sharing love. And that could look very small, and it could look very big, and it could look everywhere in between.'[13]

With around 2 billion members,[14] the Church has immense potential to spark goodness in the world and live out its mission of holistic transformation. Think about that staggering number of followers of Jesus! Instead of feeling parched, we can nurture hope, build connections and make an impact, much like a rewilding growing forest, where each expression of care contributes to the well-being of God's creation and humanity.

My journey with the Renew Our World movement

Several years ago, I had the privilege to be part of the founding group of leaders for the Renew Our World movement. In this role, I collaborated with many contributors who were interviewed for this book. It is an example of holistic transformation because it is shaping people and praying and acting for climate justice. The beauty of this growing network lies in its ability to take on different forms in different countries, welcoming people to participate.[15] From diverse places, Christians rally fellow believers and join forces to stand up, speak out and act boldly. Renew Our World is just one example of what can be achieved by the Church in response to the climate crisis. It spans continents – from Australia to vibrant Brazil, from India to the Emerald Isles of Ireland, from Malawi's warmth to Mozambique's coast, from the Netherlands to Nigeria, from Peru to the UK, and from the USA to the majestic sunsets of Zambia. Behind the scenes, global Christian organisations catalyse and co-ordinate like an empowering root system, and those organisations, in turn, are enabled by thousands of ordinary supporters giving and living faithfully. In some places, Christians lead the charge, lobbying governments, advocating for systemic change, championing plastic-free oceans with impactful campaigns, and planting trees. In other contexts, theology shifts – towards creation justice and practical lifestyle changes. And so the movement has surged and grown to more than twenty countries. In unity, there is strength; in action, hope.

As we confront the challenges of climate change, we do so with the expectation that the Holy Spirit will move in power. I had one such encounter with God at a house of prayer with Renew Our World advocates.

The chapel's stone walls glowed warmly in the last rays of the sun, casting long shadows across the grass. As we stepped inside, leaving the wind to howl over the rugged Welsh hills, a sense of sacredness enveloped us. A small group of five from the UK and Australia had gathered for a common cause. We were in the start-up phase, aiming to ignite a global movement of care for God's world. After months of working online with diverse leaders from Peru, India, Zambia and beyond, a small group of us meeting face to face was new territory.

Settling into the cosy sanctuary, we felt a connection that transcended our differences. One of our group began to sing; her voice was pure and beautiful. We joined in with songs of praise, shared stories of faith, prayed for one another and broke bread. We felt the presence of God among us, reinforcing our courage and determination. It didn't matter where we came from or what our backgrounds were. We were united by our faith in action.

We shared a vision of God renewing our world, healing its wounds and restoring its beauty, and felt the call to join in this work: to be his hands and feet in our broken world. We all had stories from our growing movement of Christians who were living differently, praying fervently and speaking boldly for change. We recalled the story of our colleagues far away in Nigeria, who led young eco-warriors to transform their communities and churches with passion and creativity. They used music, poetry and art to raise awareness and action on environmental issues, reaching widely through national radio.

I shared about my experience representing our movement at the United Nations climate talks in Germany the week before. I was initially filled with a mix of excitement and apprehension, anticipating feelings of overwhelm, jet lag and fear. Yet I found myself feeling both fulfilled and fearless, due to how God opened so many doors. Meeting with world leaders and advocating for the global Church was a powerful experience. I felt truly blessed to use my skills for a greater purpose, transitioning from engaging in discussions during the day to lifting up prayers at night. It was heartening to see so many people join together in prayer, seeking courage, wisdom and compassion for the negotiators, and asking for breakthroughs to move beyond the stalemates at the talks. Knowing that so many were standing with the small lobbying team I was part of in a round-the-clock prayer vigil created a sense of hope and unity that was palpable.

Our colleagues from the UK explained how they were exploring theology and zero-waste lifestyles with their friends, seeing these as acts of worship and stewardship. They challenged consumerism and materialism and sought to live more simply and generously.

We shared accounts received from church leaders in India who were learning about creation care theology and applying it to their contexts. They were developing action plans to reduce their environmental footprint, adopting climate-resilient farming practices with marginalised communities, and praying. We heard from campaigners in Malawi who were fighting in the courts to ban plastic bags, which were polluting their land and water. We were inspired by stories from Christian forest protectors in Ghana who were resisting mining interests, illegal logging and wildlife poaching. They were defending their ancestral lands and God's creatures from exploitation and destruction.

These stories filled us with awe and gratitude. This was what a diverse group of us across continents had dreamed of when we collaborated through our respective organisations and started Renew Our World. But we never imagined how much God would do through his people – how he would multiply these efforts and bless our work.

And as a handful of us sat in the chapel, surrounded by candlelight, we read from Jesus' words in Matthew 5:14–16:

> You are the light of the world. A town built on a hill cannot be hidden. Neither do people light a lamp and put it under a bowl. Instead they put it on its stand, and it gives light to everyone in the house. In the same way, let your light shine before others, that they may see your good deeds and glorify your Father in heaven.

We felt God speaking to us through these words. God was calling us to be his light in the world, to shine love and truth wherever we went, embracing action and good deeds. God was calling us to share our stories with others, to inspire and encourage those around us to join in. God was calling us to work for transformation through his Church.

Leaving the chapel, I knew that this experience of fellowship and prayer had changed us. We had seen a glimpse of God's kingdom on earth, where people of every nation and tongue worship in spirit and truth, using our God-given gifts and aligned to God's ways. This was a beautiful vision of the Church engaged in holistic transformation. We had been inspired and empowered to continue our mission, to spread God's light and love to the world.

Stepping into advocacy: a story to inspire and follow

Our next example of holistic transformation is about stepping into advocacy and engaging with fellow believers in speaking truth to power. It shows how God works through the Church and uses these faithful acts for our own spiritual renewal and shaping. In social movements and our actions, there can come a moment when we shift from a place of fearful powerlessness to one of hopeful agency and divine empowerment. In these instances, I am often reminded of Esther from the Old Testament and the words of Mordecai: 'for such a time as this' (Esther 4:14). Esther teaches us that following God requires us to speak up in crucial moments, even when we are nervous and it comes at a cost to ourselves. And when we do so, God is at work.

This is one of my Esther stories, and I hope it inspires others.

I squared my shoulders and looked around the grand marble foyer of my country's Parliament House. There, gathered under the Micah coalition banner, were hundreds of believers ready to advocate for those living in global poverty and to call for the rebuilding of foreign aid commitments. This was democracy in action, an expression of Christian love, and I felt proud and hopeful about what God would achieve through us.

For many gathered that day, it was their first venture into politics, filled with excitement and faith-fuelled courage. They were well prepared to advocate for the voiceless with grace and love.

Naomi, a young advocate, felt the weight of the moment. She was there as a voice for change, her hands trembling as she clutched her notes. Motivated by memories of poverty she had witnessed during backpacking travels, she felt the contrast between that experience and the luxury surrounding her now.

The meeting was a respectful exchange between constituents and a seasoned politician. Naomi's group presented their case with passion, and to their surprise, the politician listened attentively. While government policy didn't alter overnight, he found their unity and selflessness refreshing – a welcome change from the usual self-serving lobbying.

As Naomi and her companions emerged from the meeting, they were transformed. Their initial trepidation had given way to a sense of accomplishment and hope. They had spoken truth to power, not with polished rhetoric, but with the authenticity of their convictions. It might have been just a small step in the grand scheme, but for Naomi it was a giant leap in her journey of faith and advocacy.

This is the Church responding with a holistic expression, speaking out for justice and engaging with the world's challenges. This step into advocacy symbolises a growing movement worldwide, where people of faith engage in public spaces to advocate for the marginalised, express discipleship in integrated ways and contribute small acts towards significant change.

Kuki's story of influencing Christians to care about poverty and creation

We now turn our attention to Mizoram in north-east India, a case study of what it can look like to influence fellow Christians towards holistic transformation and see God igniting diverse expressions across the country. Kuki Rokhum inspires the Church to care for creation and advocate for justice. Consider how her story may resonate with your context.

Kuki's a trailblazer. She is the inaugural leader of Church Engagement for A Rocha International beyond the UK's borders. Her leadership journey includes breaking down barriers as the first female director within the Indian agency EFICOR's (Evangelical Fellowship of India Commission on Relief) leadership team. There, she dedicated two decades to human development and advocacy work, serving marginalised communities.[16]

Kuki's journey influencing the Indian Church is a testament to the transformative power of faith in action. Her leadership in countless church workshops has ignited a theological awakening, fostering a comprehensive gospel vision that embraces all creation. This shift has led to tangible changes, such as local churches abandoning plastic burning in favour of sustainable steps. In north-east India, she witnessed a pivotal moment when a pastor who regularly felled trees for church festival tents changed his ways. Kuki has supported churches in adopting sustainable practices such as tree planting, area clean-ups and environmental youth education. She has equipped people to advocate to local governments, amplifying the Church's role in societal change.[17]

A particularly poignant memory for Kuki involves a landless church community in a poor neighbourhood in Bihar transforming its limited space with potted plants, contributing small amounts to air-quality improvement despite their constraints. She has seen communities that are themselves in poverty discover their resources, using local bamboo to construct bridges across swollen rivers to ensure children's access to school despite floods. Kuki's stories of Christian empowerment extend to Nepal, where a village church crafted stretchers to transport the ill across challenging terrain for medical aid. In Jharkhand, she observed local churches bridging divided tribal communities through peacemaking and cultural defiance, such as attending weddings despite social and tribal barriers, and learning how to share land and forest stewardship.

These stories reflect Kuki's passion and highlight the Church's capacity in different communities in India and Nepal to embody God's kingdom's values, even in adversity. Kuki's recounting of these moments in our interview shone with the joy of witnessing churches living out their faith in meaningful, community-enhancing ways. It shows how God has worked in and through Kuki to shape people, share the word, engage in social action and enable the Church in various ways to achieve true transformation.

Case studies of faith in action at an institutional level

The following brief case studies help us imagine what is possible when we act together at institutional levels. We see holistic mission as the Church expressed through Eco Church, when churches of different sizes and denominations use their resources to take action and care for the earth, or through the international ecumenical Season of Creation each September when vast parts of the Church join together in prayer, conversation and commitment to care for our common home, or through mission expressed through faith-led development of Farmer Managed Natural Regeneration renewing communities and regreening landscapes. These institutional-scale expressions reflect our God-given wherewithal for collective efforts and the rejuvenating power of actions together.

Churches using their resources through the Eco Church scheme

The Eco Church scheme is an encouraging example of an integrated approach to what the Church is, does and says.[18] From preaching to installing solar panels and establishing community gardens, many churches and denominations are leveraging their resources to make a tangible impact. Ruth Valerio, our theologian and contributor from earlier, played a key role in launching the Eco Church initiative. She is heartened by the involvement of five thousand churches in the UK and beyond, fostering momentum for environmental and social justice. The scheme guides churches and denominations in integrating creation care into their worship and daily practices, leading to building audits, reduced carbon footprints and strengthened faith.[19] It is an excellent example of churches and their institutions acting in a co-ordinated and impactful way and focusing on practical behaviour change with buy-in at a local level. The Eco Church scheme is a way not only to measure and improve the environmental performance of churches, but also to witness to and share the gospel with others. It may be that your local church is ready to explore steps like these, or you could begin by inspiring people and holding some services outdoors. Ruth believes this fosters a much-needed connection between the congregation's love of nature and their Christian faith as an integral part of worshipping the Lord of all creation.[20]

Season of Creation changing Sunday worship

Incorporating environmental concerns into our prayers and liturgies in our Sunday services is part of the integral task of the Church, and this has been taken up worldwide at denominational and local levels through Season of Creation. Combining word and deed as an expression of holistic mission, this ecumenical movement invites all Christians to celebrate and care for God's creation in September every year. Its growth is an encouraging sign of God's spiritual renewal at work through the Church. It involves various activities that churches optionally draw from, such as prayer services, liturgies, readings and environmental actions. There is no shortage of resources to inspire worshipping communities to get involved.[21] Some of the leaders of Season of Creation are Dave Bookless, whom we met earlier, and Rachel Mash, the leader of Green Anglicans.

Green Anglicans is a youth movement that also expresses mission holistically, forges local expressions of Season of Creation and champions practical action. It grew out of the Anglican Church of Southern Africa. Rachel is tireless in inspiring and equipping people across Africa and beyond to preach, teach and act for God's world.[22] Green Anglicans produces preaching outlines and youth and children's resources, and mobilises people to plant trees, clean up rivers and join climate strikes. In the coming years, there will be a significant focus across Africa and the broader Anglican Communion internationally on growing trees and ecosystem restoration, with an ambitious denominational goal through The Communion Forest initiative.[23] These are encouraging signs of renewal and of the Church living out its transformative mission.

Forest and mindset regeneration transforming lives and landscapes

We can witness God at work through remarkable changes as the Church engages in holistic mission by implementing faith-led initiatives that address poverty and restore creation. One such expression is the revolutionary forest underground movement catalysed by missionary and agronomist Tony Rinaudo in Niger in the 1980s and expanded through World Vision. This is an incredible nature-based, low-cost solution to climate change and food insecurity that learns from God's wisdom and works with nature, unlocking the hidden potential of dry and barren lands to grow millions of trees. Also known as Farmer Managed Natural Regeneration (FMNR), this approach restores local ecosystems by empowering farmers to prune and manage growth from germinating seeds, tree stumps and roots to re-establish trees on cleared land. Increased tree cover helps lower temperatures for farming and local communities, buffering climatic extremes and benefiting nearby areas. Local biodiversity returns with animal habitat, shelter and food sources. It is a testimony to the power of nature to heal itself and a story of empowering people to change destructive tree-cutting practices. The knowledge and techniques that began with Tony Rinaudo have spread voluntarily from farmer to farmer, and with World Vision's championing now reach over forty countries across Africa, Asia and Latin America. In Niger Republic alone, over a twenty-year period the FMNR movement has led to 200 million trees regenerated across 5 million hectares of degraded farmland.[24] That's a lot of trees and rapid regeneration!

The forest underground movement not only helps restore ecosystems and enable people to grow food, but it also teaches an inspiring lesson about changing mindsets. It emphasises the importance of accepting responsibility for one's future and collaborating towards a common goal. Tony has witnessed people transform their perspectives and become more open to trying new approaches, which he believes is essential for taking action on climate change. He finds great value in encouraging people to use their imagination by reflecting on how the environment used to support them in their subsistence farming, comparing it with the current situation, and contemplating what might happen if we continue with business as usual, destroying our environment. Tony poses the question, 'What will the future hold for our children?' This process of reflection and imagination has sparked hope that changes through FMNR methods are achievable and can be effective, highlighting the importance of working together to be part of the solution. The movement grew because of this shift in mindset and methodology.[25]

The forest underground movement is a story that began with a Christian and a faith-based organisation that sought to faithfully partner with and make a difference in arid communities in famine. Church organisations have long been significant contributors to faith-based development work that celebrates the whole of life and cares for people and places. It is a model of the Christian response to God's call to transformation and good in our world.

A beautiful tomorrow

God calls the Church to be caring and loving in integrated ways, proclaiming the fullness of the gospel in word and deed. As with the exciting possibilities we imagine with rewilding, we can envision the work of the Church in fullness, alive and shaping people, sharing good news and seeking justice in our time. This is good for us, and good for our world. As we reflect on these inspiring stories, we see that every act of love and care contributes to a brighter future. The collective efforts of individuals and communities, driven by faith and compassion, create change that extends far beyond our surroundings. In a world filled with challenges, the Church can stand as a beacon of hope, demonstrating that through unity and purpose we can nurture a beautiful tomorrow. That is what it means to take God's call seriously.

Let us embrace our roles as stewards of God's creation, fostering connections and cultivating a spirit of generosity and love. Followers of Jesus are engaging in various activities to promote positive change, deeply rooted in love. The Church has immense potential to drive transformation globally, impacting communities locally and worldwide. This includes our response to the challenge of climate change, where we, the Church, can play a momentous role. Rather than feeling desolate and depleted, be encouraged and nurture fresh hope and connections. These showcased stories of faith in action highlight that there are diverse ways to lead significant change and respond to the mission of the Church. May they inspire us to play a holistic part in a just and sustainable future.

Reflection

The following is an imaginative exercise designed to explore the concept of spiritual rewilding as we look to revitalise our faith and bring new life to our churches.

Find a quiet place where you can feel comfortable.

Take some deep breaths, allowing yourself to relax in this moment.

Imagine standing in a barren, dry and lifeless landscape. Feel the dryness in the air and the emptiness around you.

Consider how this desolate land represents areas of your faith or church life that feel dry and lifeless. Reflect on which aspects of your discipleship or community lack vitality and growth.

Now visualise a gentle rain beginning to fall. Picture the drops soaking into the parched earth, nourishing it and bringing life. Imagine seeds hidden in the soil starting to sprout, with green shoots pushing through the ground. Take a moment to thank God for this new growth.

Let your mind wander to different approaches to spiritual rewilding. What comes to mind when you envision the Church as a community that shapes people, shares the word and engages in social action? Where can you imagine green shoots?

Consider how your local church could engage in meaningful action and contribute to good deeds in the community.

- Could your congregation collaborate with other organisations to address local issues such as food insecurity? Initiatives such as establishing a community garden or food pantry could be beneficial.
- You might consider offering support to students from low-income families, assisting people to navigate government or legal systems, or advocating for change by writing letters to political or business decision-makers.
- Participating in public forums or supporting ethical initiatives, community clean-ups, tree-planting events or sustainable living projects can promote just changes.
- Think about how your local church could also take part in the annual Season of Creation.

Finally, take a moment to thank God for this time and for the new life beginning to take root in your faith and community.

Lord Jesus,
We marvel at the beauty of your world, where nature transforms barren landscapes into vibrant life.
Inspire us to rewild our hearts and communities.
May our churches be places that shape hearts, share your word, and engage boldly and holistically with the world around us.
Ignite our imaginations with visions of a Church that reflects your justice and love.
With conviction and enthusiasm, we say, 'Amen. Come, Lord Jesus.'
We know we are capable of being agents of transformation.
Empower us to unite in this crucial mission of healing and renewal.
Bless our offerings and amplify their impact.
With your help, we can make a difference.
Amen.

Part 2

3

Call: describing and naming the problem

> The era of global warming is over . . . the era of global boiling has arrived.
> (United Nations chief António Guterres)[1]

As we grapple with the escalating impact of climate change, the urgent warning from António Guterres, the Secretary-General of the United Nations regarding 'global boiling' cannot be ignored. Take a moment to reflect on how this message makes you feel. It's normal to have mixed emotions when confronting such a significant issue. You may feel sceptical, not just about the efficacy of international organisations like the United Nations in tackling these challenges, but also about the notion of 'global boiling' itself. Or perhaps you're feeling numb or overwhelmed by the sheer scale of the problem and the magnitude of the response it demands. You might even cycle through multiple different feelings – anger, fear, hopelessness or a motivated urgency to act. Whatever your reaction, it is a valid starting point for engaging in this vital global conversation.

To hear the call for climate action we must first name the problems. Crucial steps for us to accept climate risk involve calling out the brokenness of our high-consumption global systems, and acknowledging the place of the Western Church and the need to engage at all levels of faith and society. While some people resist the call, others are burdened with eco-anxiety. The discipline of lament and the sacred pause offered by Easter Saturday help us hold the grief from climate change's damage while also nurturing a sense of hope.

We are in a climate crisis because human activity, particularly in the last two hundred years, has led to a rapid increase of carbon dioxide (CO_2) and other greenhouse gases in our atmosphere. While the last two centuries saw extraordinary improvements in human health and productive capacity, and a profound reshuffle in people's economic positions, the Industrial Revolution ushered in our use of fossil fuels. What previous generations did not understand, though, was the environmental cost.

Due to the increasing levels of CO_2 in the atmosphere from burning fossil fuels such as coal, oil and gas, as well as deforestation and industrial agriculture, the earth's thermostat cannot manage the extra heat. As a result, global temperatures have risen, putting significant stress on the earth's systems. At the time I write this (2024), the global average temperature is 1.1°C above pre-industrial levels, and it is likely that temperatures will temporarily exceed 1.5°C above pre-industrial levels within the next five years.[2] Some of the consequences of this strain include more extreme rainfall events, which damage homes and crops; more frequent and more intense heatwaves; the potential for more prolonged and more intense droughts, causing water shortages and disease; more destructive bushfires; more warming and acidification of oceans, affecting fish, reefs and coastal communities; increased threats to food production, leading to hunger; and melting ice and glaciers, raising sea levels and flooding low-lying areas. Climate scientists are gravely concerned that our natural world is reaching a tipping point. For instance, in the Arctic, melting frozen soil is releasing methane, ice at the poles and mountains is disappearing, and changing ocean currents and temperatures are impacting salinity.

To address climate change and keep warming within safer limits of 1.5°C above pre-industrial levels we must reduce greenhouse gas emissions. Our world leaders agreed in 2015 in the UN Paris Climate Agreement for pathways to bring down humanity's greenhouse gas emissions by almost half by 2030, with levels down to net zero by 2050.[3] This transformation is essential for fostering climate-resilient development and justice.[4] Accelerated transformative action is needed, and the longer humanity delays, the more loss and damage there will be.

Climate change places a heavy burden on our global community, making essential resources such as water, food and arable land increasingly scarce. This leads to heightened conflicts, displacement of people, deteriorating health and threats to social cohesion. Climate change acts as a threat multiplier, exacerbating existing issues and generating new challenges. The stories we will explore in the next chapter reflect the experiences of individuals in various locations, all united by the pain and grief that accompany changes in the natural world. It is crucial to understand that this suffering affects us all, and we cannot observe it indifferently.

All of us must engage with uncomfortable information about the climate emergency as a global challenge that requires global solutions, and we must grasp that the moment for our generation to act is now. Previous generations did not understand our problems or the harmful consequences, but our generation knows and can do something about it. There is a rapidly narrowing window of opportunity to transform our ways and transition our world systems to safe levels and lower climate risk. When I refer to 'our generation', I mean everyone living on our planet now. Whether we were born in 1980 and anticipate our seventieth birthday in 2050, or were born in 2020 with that milestone in 2090, the extent to which we and future generations will experience a significantly hotter world – whether under very high or low emissions[5] – depends on how we tackle the climate challenge today. We are all facing the same global realities, not limited by narrow age demographics. For future generations, it will be too late to start taking action. The time to act is now, and it must begin earnestly with our generation. Instead of feeling overwhelmed, let's take a moment to focus and truly listen. What better topic to concentrate on right now than the stories and ideas shared in this book?

At this point, we have to face up to a hard truth, which is that the Western Church is complicit in global economic and climate injustice. This complicity has damaged discipleship so that in many parts of the Western Church, climate change is ignored or dismissed as politically partisan and not core business. In some cases, this is a sin of omission; however, in other instances – perhaps where political polarisation has become prominent – it is a sin of commission. How has this happened? Have we lost sight of what we are saved for?

To begin to address these questions, we will seek to understand the role of our global systems and culture, particularly when those economic systems and consumerism hurt others. This will prompt us to ask further questions: to reflect on our priorities and choices and those of our churches and organisations. Let us create a space to listen to the stirring of the Holy Spirit and see things anew. As the body of Christ (1 Corinthians 12:12), each of us has a role to play in addressing the harm caused by the climate crisis.

Insatiable growth hits environmental limits

It's easy to forget that we live in a world with God-given limits. Yet we are now stretching beyond the earth's natural boundaries, with extreme poverty and inequality on the rise. While God gifted humanity an abundant world within natural limits, true abundance and our call to stewardship do not mean endlessly extracting and accumulating resources. Our global high-consumption economic systems are broken and not functioning as God intended.

Human beings have essential life needs, starting with food, water and shelter. You may think of other vital needs that are missing from this list, such as healthcare, education, work and more. Consider our primary human needs as a social foundation below which we do not want to fall.[6] The injustice in our world is that the resources to meet our essential life needs are not shared fairly. You may already know that the world's richest 1% have as much wealth as the rest of the world combined.[7] It's pretty staggering. Added to that, the same wealthy 1% of the world's population create more than double the amount of carbon pollution of the poorest 50%.[8] As we have heard, people living in poverty bear the brunt of damaging consequences. The rest of us fall somewhere in the middle – not the worst and not the best. When some people have so little and a few have so much, we must change our systems to fairer and more sustainable practices to address these inequalities.

Visualise the shape of a ring doughnut. This is how Oxford economist Kate Raworth illustrates that our world has limits to how much it can sustain human activities and environmental changes, requiring safe operating boundaries. She rejects the frame of endless growth and proposes a twenty-first-century sustainable economy within our earth's limits that enables both human and non-human life to thrive.[9] The boundaries incorporate a social foundation of people's basic needs and an ecological ceiling within which to safely exist. Tearfund engaged with some of these ideas in a discussion paper called 'The Restorative Economy'[10] and grappled with God's vision for an economy where we shift towards living within environmental limits, work towards ensuring that everyone can meet their basic needs and keep inequality within reasonable bounds. It urged the Church to be at the forefront of living a different story and working to restore that which is broken.

The concept of planetary boundaries is a set of nine scientific limits within which humanity can safely continue to operate and thrive for generations. This concept was developed by scientists Johan Rockström, Will Steffen and others at Stockholm University. As of 2023, their analysis concluded that we have transgressed six of the nine boundaries.[11] Take a moment to let that sink in. We have crossed the thresholds in six out of the nine planetary boundaries which are carefully set in our natural world by our wise Creator God. These limits include freshwater change, land-use change, our biosphere and climate change. This is alarming because, as the study shows,

> Crossing boundaries increases the risk of generating large-scale abrupt or irreversible environmental changes. Drastic changes will not necessarily happen overnight, but together the boundaries mark a critical threshold for increasing risks to people and the ecosystems we are part of.[12]

Our world is under immense strain, and the structure of our global economic systems needs to be revised. Some of our biggest corporations don't follow the same rules as the rest of us, making profits unjustly, avoiding taxes, harming our environment or underpaying employees. Too often, our governments have neglected their duty to ensure that everyone in society is taken care of. Too often, our desire for wealth and power has been left unchecked.

Whether we are aware of it or not, we are interconnected with larger economic systems. The English-speaking world's favourite nature broadcaster, Sir David Attenborough, explains,

> We are all culpable but, it has to be said, through no fault of our own. It is only in the last few decades that we have come to understand that every one of us has been born into a human world that was always inherently unsustainable. But now that we know this, we have a choice to make. We could carry on living our happy lives, raising our families, busying ourselves with the honest pursuits of the modern society that we have built, whilst choosing to disregard the disaster waiting on our doorstep. Or we could change.[13]

How could we possibly change the brokenness of our global economic systems? We will briefly look at the possibility of large-scale change at this point and return to it towards the end of this book. Understanding systemic brokenness allows us to imagine new possibilities and advocate for justice and systemic change. Christiana Figueres, the lead negotiator of the 2015 UN Paris Climate Agreement, explains,

> Paradoxically, systemic change is a deeply personal endeavor. Our social and economic structures are a product of our way of thinking. For example, our economy is based on the belief that we can extract resources boundlessly, use them inefficiently, and discard them wantonly, drawing from the planet more than it can regenerate and polluting more than we

> can clean up. Over time we've developed a deeply exploitative ethos as the basis of our actions. This no longer works.[14]

As we reflect on these systemic challenges, consider what it could mean to stand up for change. In the next section, we will explore the Church's role and responsibility in the face of global crises.

Where is the Church?

Many churches in wealthy Western cultures have ignored the problems of environmental damage and social injustice. These matters are not seen as important or are deemed too political. The political dimension of climate change, entangled in partisan culture wars and policy stalemates, further complicates the Church's response. Often, the Western Church lacks awareness, fears compromising the gospel, and either gives low priority to creation and justice issues or outright denies them. This neglect extends to the history of domination of places and peoples, as well as the impact of industrialisation. These forces have altered how humans relate to nature and one another, resulting in modern forms of power and resource abuse, habitat loss and environmental crises. Western culture, influenced by the Enlightenment and other philosophical movements, has fostered a sense of detachment and independence from nature among people and separation of the secular from the sacred.[15] Such cultural ideas have also shaped and influenced the Church over time.

This individualistic approach neglects our collective responsibility in an interconnected world. N. T. Wright warns against ignoring the world and pursuing private salvation. He urges us to hear the 'call to follow Jesus and become part of his plan to sort out the world now, as much as we can, in advance of the final day'.[16] Similarly, theologian Chris Wright calls out forces of idolatry such as wealth, greed, power and success that entice the Western Church away from faithfully living out God's call.[17] Aboriginal elder Uncle Ray Minniecon rebukes the Western Church for leading us down a theological path that champions individualism, constricting God's broader mandate to care for our neighbours, both near and far.[18] Let's take a moment to contemplate how our actions towards our global neighbours align with our Christian calling.

The parable of the Good Samaritan (Luke 10:25–37) illustrates Jesus' teachings on proactive love and the identification of our neighbour. A man journeying from Jerusalem to Jericho fell victim to robbers and was left wounded on the roadside. While a priest and a Levite passed by the man in need without a second glance, it was a Samaritan, hailing from a different ethnic background and homeland, who recognised the gravity of the situation. Struck by a profound concern and care, the Samaritan stopped to help and demonstrated remarkable compassion. With a generous spirit, he devoted both time and resources to aid the man, embodying Jesus' teaching of what it means to love our neighbour.

In this parable, Jesus calls us to show to our neighbours loving care which stems from our devotion and obedience to God. As the passage in Luke begins, we are instructed, '"Love the Lord your God with all your heart and with all your soul and with all your strength and with all your mind"; and, "Love your neighbour as yourself"' (Luke 10:27). How might we embody this teaching to aid those affected by our current global challenges? Uncle Ray urges us to elevate our practical expressions of love in proportion to the scale of harm, cautioning, 'We're too placid in responding to the urgency of the climate crisis.'[19]

On this topic, I interviewed two leaders whom I greatly respect, each with distinct but overlapping areas of expertise: Professor Katharine Hayhoe and Revd Dr Dave Bookless.

Katharine's story

Katharine Hayhoe has a remarkable track record of reaching out to Christians and the broader society in polarised settings. She is a world-renowned climate scientist, United Nations Champion of the Earth, World Evangelical Alliance Ambassador, academic and communicator. Katharine's a bit of a Christian hero of mine. She communicates persuasively and effectively using media, speaking and writing to get the message out, and she has reached millions through her public platforms.

Katharine encourages the Church to be at the forefront of climate action, rather than absent. She emphasises that the Bible is rich with references to nature and God's care for the lilies of the field. Ignoring the natural world, she argues, is a tremendous lost opportunity and a tragic witness to non-believers, potentially driving them away from the Church.[20]

As a Canadian based in Texas, USA, Katharine regularly encounters vehement objections from American Christians to the reality of climate change. She traces evangelical history in the USA, noting how culture has evolved to link religion with political ideology and objectives. This merger of ideology with Christianity has now gained influence worldwide. Katharine distinguishes the objections to climate change as 'theological sounding and pious, religious or even Christian in tone, but when you open your Bible, you see that they're not actually there'.[21] In her interview, Katharine pointed out that in the complexity and polarisation of the USA, 40% of people who identify as evangelical don't go to church, and what's influencing them is 'politics pure and simple'.[22] Polarisation and extreme right-wing ideology have skyrocketed, and Katharine describes them as having infected the Church as well as societies from the USA to Canada, Australia, the UK and Europe.

There are many perspectives on climate change in the worldwide Church. Dave Bookless, whom we met earlier, deeply appreciates these differing views.

Dave's story

Dave is a true gentleman, with bird-watching binoculars, who is graciously interested in the lives of those around him while tirelessly shaping and teaching the global Church on creation care. Dave's influence extends far and wide. He is a husband, father, parish priest, author, international theologian and global leader in environmental care. And he loves watching and studying birds. Dave serves as the longstanding international head of theology for A Rocha, a conservation organisation that helps care for God's creation in more than twenty countries worldwide. Dave leads an international gospel and creation care movement as Lausanne Catalyst for Creation Care. He shared his wisdom contributing to this book while cooking vegetarian curry for me in his London vicarage.

Dave suggests that it is more cultural and political than biblical to object to engaging with climate change. He finds that climate change is a no-go area in some parts of the Church and not a problem to engage with in other parts among Christians who believe the same things. Dave has found that some people in the Global North are resistant because they are terrified about what will happen if their economies, and their prosperity – built entirely on fossil fuels – get challenged: 'You see an argument only in rich countries and, almost inevitably, the ones most dependent on fossil fuels. So it can't be about theology. It's got to be about politics and culture. Yes, perhaps about sin.'[23]

James Bhagwan agrees with this point, diagnosing, 'At the heart of the ecological crisis, there's a spiritual sickness.'[24] Many of us reading this book live in contexts where selfish desires have run rampant, allowing insatiable consumption and extraction in economic systems that can feel inevitable and unchangeable. As Christians and churches in these contexts, we must not mindlessly exist in consumerism and these systems while ignoring the damage to others and our natural world. It's time for change.

A good life for everyone can be our shared goal. And when we recognise that some self-interested corporations and forces get in the way of that goal, we can do something about it. We can lean towards equal and fair solutions to restore the balance between people and our planet. We can urge and agitate for accountable governments to keep systems and corporations in check for the benefit of all.[25] Let's choose to recover from the spiritual sickness at the heart of our ecological crisis and embrace lives that are kind to our natural world and fellow human beings.

'At the heart of the ecological crisis, there's a spiritual sickness.' (James Bhagwan)

Faith and climate action: engaging younger generations

Younger people of faith are prioritising concern for climate change. However, many are leaving the Church in Western contexts due to disengagement. Research by Tearfund and Youthscape found that '9 out of 10 Christian young people are concerned about climate change. Just 1 out of 10 think their Church is doing enough about it.'[26] In Australia, Tearfund and NCLS Research found mixed levels of Christian engagement with climate change, with relative silence alienating young people. More than three in five Christians aged 18–40 report being 'very or extremely concerned'[27] about climate change. The younger the Christians, the more concerned they are likely to be, and many perceive a generational divide on the issue.[28] They want to see the Church engaging more in conversation and action around climate change in ways that connect with their faith.

As some churches in some countries become more divided along political lines, people leave because they don't see engagement with (or even acknowledgement of) the issues affecting their world. It is an entirely good and appropriate thing to seek to connect faith and current challenges as we strive to live and follow Jesus, who is the Way, Truth and Life (John 14:6). Christians who are disappointed with the local church tend to either drift away or find a new home in groups and networks that share their faith and passion. Those who find community often join Christian organisations, student communities and grassroots movements that help them live out their faith through action.

The conviction of younger generations to urgently act for a safer climate future demonstrates care for their future and generations to come. The themes of future generations and creation resonate with our role as caretakers of God's world. Psalm 78 implores us to remember and keep God's ways, teaching our children

so that the next generation would know them,
even the children yet to be born,
and they in turn would tell their children.
(Psalm 78:6)

Psalm 104 highlights God's wisdom and provision for all creation; Psalm 145 tells of one generation commending God's works to another (Psalm 145:4); and Deuteronomy 28 describes the blessings of obedience yet despair and destruction when we do not follow God's ways.

Addressing a safer climate future inherently requires involvement in political processes. The transitions needed to create safer and more equitable systems demand co-ordinated, large-scale policy changes and collective action. Engaging in political efforts to tackle climate change aligns with Christian values by emphasising creation care, advocating for the vulnerable and striving for the common good. This involvement enables followers of Jesus to make a positive impact in our world, and younger generations can lead the way for older ones.

Many Christians feel uneasy about engaging with politics or may not want to acknowledge its impact on faith and life. Finding the right balance is important. We need churches that integrate engagement on topics such as climate change theologically and respond practically, including with political engagement. It's imperative not to choose a local church based on political alignment, as it may divert us from the gospel. At the same time, churches should not simply adopt the prevailing philosophical or political views, as this can also lead to troubling outcomes. Instead, we should approach issues affecting our world first from a biblical perspective rather than assuming a political one, and cultivate a mindset of humble listening and loving faith responses. In his book *A Mucky Business*, prominent Christian UK politician Tim Farron emphasises the significance of Christians integrating faith and active political participation.[29] Indeed, we need only look at Old Testament leaders such as Moses, David and Esther, and civil servants Joseph or Daniel, to see examples of individuals grappling with similar issues. Tim Farron urges us to follow the example of Jesus by immersing ourselves in the complexity and working from within the world to bring about positive change. And when we apply our beliefs to solve challenges that affect everyone, we demonstrate love for our neighbours.

A congregation learning to 'disagree agreeably'

What does constructive dialogue on divisive issues such as justice and climate change look like? When I asked Katharine Hayhoe when she'd seen the Church at its best, she gave the example of Grace Capital City in Washington, D.C. as a church learning to disagree agreeably.[30] Pastor Chris Moerman and his wife, Jessica Moerman, a climate scientist who heads the Evangelical Environmental Network, guide their church in justice and creation care. Embracing a non-dogmatic approach, the church attracts political staffers from both major parties, fostering discussions rooted in faith and love rather than political ideologies. Katharine has been a guest speaker and praises the church for fostering open conversations. She sees it as a beacon of the Church's true mission: uniting people in love and shared values.[31] Additionally, the church actively participates in practical efforts such as river clean-ups and local environmental partnerships.[32] This commitment to dialogue and environmental stewardship is echoed by Christians in other partisan contexts who seek to engage with political issues and find common ground.

The Church has a crucial opportunity to engage in climate action rather than getting caught up in partisan politics or remaining silent. Ignoring our responsibility is dangerous and underscores the substantial impact that culture and politics have on our responses. We should acknowledge the passionate appeals of young people as prophetic calls that urge portions of the Western Church to break free from inertia and seize missed opportunities.

Eco-anxiety and lament

'Though the mountains be shaken
  and the hills be removed,

yet my unfailing love for you will not be shaken
nor my covenant of peace be removed,'
says the LORD, who has compassion on you.
(Isaiah 54:10)

Some people choose to avoid engaging with the issue of climate change, while others experience anxiety, fear and even despair. If you find yourself feeling overwhelmed, it's important to know that you are not alone. How can we cope with these emotions? One approach is to embrace the biblical practice of lament and reach out to God for support.[33] In this section, we will recognise the phenomenon of eco-anxiety and investigate how lament and prayer can help cultivate perseverance and hope.

During my interview with Katharine Hayhoe, she noted that anxiety and frustration about global events are understandable, especially among younger people who feel the present and future weight of the environmental crisis.[34] The American Psychological Association defines eco-anxiety as 'a chronic fear of environmental doom'.[35] While such feelings can motivate action, they can also lead to distress, highlighting the importance of adaptive coping strategies such as problem-solving, social support and proactive behaviour.[36] The good news is there is much we can do collectively to shape our future.[37] Katharine encourages discussions on how to make a difference, emphasising that conversations about climate change are vital. Her book *Saving Us*[38] offers strategies for effective communication. She highlights that our actions can also benefit others, stating, 'When we do something to make a difference in their lives, that helps us too.'[39] Finding safe spaces and supportive people is crucial for overcoming eco-anxiety. We have already explored how a growing body of Christians, particularly younger generations, feel frustrated with parts of the Church that resist environmental engagement. Reconnecting with like-minded individuals can empower you to take collective action. Katharine suggests seeking out Christian organisations and campaigns that promote faith and love through tangible efforts. If you feel overwhelmed raising environmental awareness in a resistant church community, it may be that another person needs to take up the call. As Paul said in 1 Corinthians 3:6, 'I planted the seed, Apollos watered it, but God has been making it grow.' Trust that God will nurture the right messengers to inspire action in his Church.

Our faith and Scriptures guide us through the pain of our broken world, offering hope and perspective. As Katharine explains, 'Our faith provides answers in a world filled with sin and suffering. We shouldn't expect everyone to love us for it, but we shouldn't surrender to fear; God did not give us a spirit of fear (2 Timothy 1:7).' Katharine admits, 'Often I feel fear, but I've come to understand that I just need to know what's the next thing for me to do.'[40] She describes her faith and renewed heart as instruments that reveal God's calling, situation by situation. 'It's a growth experience for me to depend on God during these circumstances,' she says. 'We're not called to save the world; we're called to do what he asks and trust him with the results.'[41]

> 'Often I feel fear, but I've come to understand that I just need to know what's the next thing for me to do.'
> (Katharine Hayhoe)

I resonate with Katharine's approach to faithful obedience. When engaging Christians in various campaigns, I've often been asked about the likelihood of success. While campaigns aim for specific changes, the focus should remain on faithfulness to God's call. Holly-Anna Peterson echoes this sentiment in her contribution to Hannah Malcolm's moving collection *Words for a Dying World*.[42] Peterson combines her experience as a founding member of the non-violent direct-action movement Christian Climate Action and her work in mental health. She describes the eventual balance we must strike between urgent realities and practical steps and says that the phrase 'faithful, not successful' motivates climate activists without settling for less.[43]

Scripture expresses deep anguish and lament, inviting us to emulate Jesus, who experienced sorrow. The poetry and deep emotions of the Psalms and Lamentations, alongside centuries of liturgical tradition, provide a sanctuary for articulating our lament. Lament acknowledges pain while seeking God's comfort and guidance, expressed in Lamentations 3:19–23 as affliction and a downcast soul calling to mind the hope that

> Because of the Lord's great love we are not consumed,
> for his compassions never fail.
> They are new every morning.
> (Lamentations 3:22–23)

As Tish Harrison Warren reassures us in *Prayer in the Night*,[44] we can allow ourselves the space and permission to feel sadness, weep and mourn, and draw on words from those who have come before us, such as the night-time prayer of Compline in the *Book of Common Prayer*. This is a prayer of quietness at the completion of the day, asking our Lord to keep watch over us, and to bless and soothe us and those who suffer.

Allowing yourself to lament and express your sorrow with those enduring the ecological crisis is a heartfelt response of care for both people and places. Hannah Malcolm explains that such grief reflects our love for what we cherish.[45] It also invites us to unite as the body of Christ with a pastoral response. Such holding is the approach encouraged by A Rocha, whose resources help local churches engage in eco-pastoral care.[46]

Eco-lament offers churches a way to process our grief over our losses together and commit climate action to prayer. When we integrate the practice of lament, we help navigate anxieties and find solace in our relationship with God and our church community. Resources from 24-7 Prayer with Renew Our World[47] and Christian Climate Action's 'Grief Circles'[48] provide tools for prayer and emotional sharing. Consider how these activities could help your church community engage. If lament becomes a discipline within our communities, it can lead to healing actions, such as local projects and safe spaces for discussion. Dave Bookless reassures us that as we engage in eco-lament, the Holy Spirit 'suffers alongside as comforter and intercessor, and yet also brings hope'.[49]

The sacred pause of Easter Saturday: active hope amid eco-anxiety and lament

How can we hold the grief from climate change's damage while also nurturing a sense of hope? On a grand scale, Easter Saturday is a day that mirrors our journey with climate grief – where we are suspended between the sorrow of Good Friday and the joy of Easter Sunday. On Easter Saturday, we pause in silence and mourning, caught between life and death. It is a space for our aching hearts to process grief and all that is lost, praying and waiting actively by the silent tomb. This time of reflection reminds us that even as creation groans, we are called to be present in both the pain and the hope.

As Christians, we understand that Easter Saturday, also known as Holy Saturday, represents the profound work of God in the depths of despair. It is a day that teaches us to hold fast to faith when all seems lost, trusting that resurrection is on the horizon. Stott reminds us that our salvation rests in faith alone, 'But in everything else we both trust God and take appropriate action.'[50] By this, he means we act and co-operate with God while we rely on his ultimate provision. We learn to live in faith, just as God's provision requires the birds to still act with forethought for their future and gather food for themselves. Stott explains,

> Jesus did not mean that God's children can sit back and do nothing, leaving God to do it all. Even forgiveness and eternal life, which (because Christ died to secure them for us) are totally free and non-contributory gifts of God, still have to be gratefully received by us. And in every other sphere it is yet more evident that we have to co-operate with God, as the birds teach us.[51]

With this in mind, we can face the environmental crises of our time with a yearning for restoration, and use our God-given insight and wherewithal for collective efforts in the power of God's grace.

Be encouraged to embrace this time of waiting as a period of active hope. It is a call to reflect on our actions, to mourn the damage we have inflicted on God's earth and to prepare for the work ahead. Just as Jesus lay in the tomb, there is life yet unseen, ready to emerge. In our climate advocacy, we, too, may feel that our efforts are buried, but we hold on to the promise that God is at work, transforming our seeds of change into blossoms of renewal.

Let us then, as on Holy Saturday, find solace in knowing that our challenges are held within God's larger story of redemption. Let us draw strength from one another and the everlasting hope Easter brings. As we wait between times, we do so with the assurance that God is at work in hope through our climate grief. In this, we find the courage to continue our journey even when burdened by eco-anxiety, knowing that our small steps contribute to the grand unfolding of God's redemptive plan for all creation.

Towards hope and action

If you are worried about the future, know that prayer and action create hope! God is sovereign and is on our side. We are not responsible for changing the world on our own. Instead of being defeated by anxiety and grief, God holds us as we abide in his loving power. As we are encouraged in John 15:4, 'Abide in me as I abide in you. Just as the branch cannot bear fruit by itself unless it abides in the vine, neither can you unless you abide in me' (NRSVA). Our everyday, ordinary lives are an offering to bear fruit. The Spirit inspires and empowers us. Dave Bookless reminds us that 'Lament is not an end in itself. It should lead to action, as God stirs us up to be the change we want to see in the world (Proverbs 3:6; 2 Chronicles 7:14).'[52]

The great news is that transformational change is possible when people work together. Change builds at all system levels when people join networks and movements. We may feel powerless in the face of vested interests and entrenched systems. However, recall how God used David, a shepherd boy, against the giant Goliath, with a sling and a stone. David could not deploy the tactics of the mighty army before him but innovated using the circumstances and tools at hand, acting courageously in faith. Marshall Ganz, the political scholar and activist, also uses David's story to remind us that through history, ordinary people can achieve extraordinary things by organising themselves, mobilising their values and using their creativity and courage.[53] Seemingly impossible change does happen, often when social movements develop their strategic capacity and build collective action with hard work and focus.

Reflection

Allow yourself some time for the following spiritual exercise to contemplate and process grief and anticipation. In Matthew 27:61, we read, 'Mary Magdalene and the other Mary were sitting there opposite the tomb', and we will use our imaginations to enter that scene of sacred waiting.

Find a quiet place to be present, and focus on slow, deep breaths as you begin.

Imagine yourself alongside Mary Magdalene and the other Mary, sitting opposite the tomb where Jesus was laid.

Feel the weight of emotion in the air.

The tomb is silent, and the world feels suspended between sorrow and hope.

Consider the sacred space you are in.

How does it feel to be in this place of waiting and contemplation?

What emotions arise as you sit by the tomb, processing grief and anticipation?

What might God be inviting you to explore or embrace in this moment?

Consider what support and compassion for one another might look like as we confront the grief and anxiety of the climate crisis together.

As you sit by the tomb, imagine God speaking to you in this moment of stillness.

What is he inviting you to explore or embrace?

How can this sacred waiting transform your understanding of hope and action?

As you return to the present and conclude this reflection, thank God for this time of sacred waiting and the hope that lies ahead.

Merciful God,
In this sacred space of waiting and hope, we bring before you our fragile hearts, burdened by eco-anxiety and the weight of the climate crisis. We cry out to you, lamenting the damage done to your creation and the suffering it brings.
How long, O Lord, will we see the earth groan under the weight of our actions?
How long will your creation suffer and your people despair?
Grant us the strength to hold on to hope, even in the midst of despair. Help us to see your hand at work, transforming our small efforts into seeds of renewal. May we find comfort in your promise of resurrection and new life.
Turn your face towards us, O Lord, and hear our plea.
Surround us with your loving compassion, and guide us to be a source of support and encouragement for one another.
In our waiting, may we actively hope and trust in your redemptive plan for all creation. As we wait in the silence of Holy Saturday, may we hold on to the hope of Easter morning and the promise of resurrection.
In Jesus' name we pray.
Amen.

4

Response: listening to global perspectives

> Ears that hear and eyes that see –
> the Lord has made them both.
> (Proverbs 20:12)

To respond to God's call to care for both people and our planet, we must listen deeply to the voices from the front lines of those affected. By engaging with perspectives from First Nations peoples and those from the Global South, we can hear their calls to reflect on our impact on the earth. This includes adopting an interconnected approach to caring for all of creation and recognising our place within it. In this chapter, we will explore some current realities and their effects: the pain of creation groaning (Romans 8:22) alongside the suffering of our fellow human beings. We will hear three accounts of climate impact from different parts of the world: from Felistar in her Maasai community in Kenya, Reverend James in the Pacific, and Uncle Ray from an Indigenous Australian perspective. These stories provide insights into the larger crisis affecting our brothers and sisters and the natural world. Your own context may differ, and you may not yet feel the impact of climate change or may have access to resources that buffer the harm. However, we cannot wait until we all experience these effects first-hand. We must listen, and we must learn.

The rivers run dry: Felistar's story

When I met Felistar, it was in Laikipia, Kenya, amid a landscape ravaged by climate change and drought. I was there as part of my international development and humanitarian efforts, but nothing could have prepared me for what I witnessed.

The riverbed was bone dry, cracked and dusty. The air was still. Ahead of me, a group of Maasai women and children walked slowly, looking for a spot to dig – a place to coax water from the reluctant earth. Their faces were weary and resigned. The usual chatter of children was conspicuously absent; they were too quiet. The natural world was fading. The landscape was close to uninhabitable, yet all clung to life.

For generations, the people and wild animals had lived alongside one another, but the drought had sharpened the edges of their coexistence into conflict. By night, elephants – gaunt shadows driven by an insatiable thirst – laid siege to any remnants of water, their tusks destroying the remaining water tanks with desperate ease. Come morning, the women would emerge to a scene of destruction, their own thirst mirroring the parched throat of the land. With resolve, they would once again gather at the cracked riverbed, delving into the earth's depths in search of moisture.

Each day's labour was a testament to hope, as small cups were used to scoop up the day's meagre water, reflecting the community's collective will. And as night reclaimed the sky, the cycle would begin anew, with the animals returning to the humans' hard-won pools, all united in the singular quest to quench an unrelenting thirst.

I was in Kenya representing my aid organisation and meeting with our local church partner to visit the different communities in which we work.[1] Our Kenyan partner had previously conducted a women's economic empowerment programme. That was how I came to meet Felistar and walk alongside her in a dry riverbed. Felistar was one of the women who had participated in the training the previous year. Back then, she had shared her story of how she had learned to keep sheep, goats and poultry, lead others in 'table banking', meaning microcredit loans in local women's groups, and how she had earned enough money to feed her family and would send her children to school. She had smiled proudly in the photos that accompanied her hopeful story.

But the Felistar I met that day seemed a shadow of her former self. The drought had taken so much from her. Her animals had died or been sold at a loss. Her small crops had withered, and her husband was far away searching for work. Her children were surviving on one cup of porridge a day, provided by our emergency feeding programme. She looked at me with hollow eyes, holding her new baby, expressing her story of struggle through the interpreter. As Felistar told her story a year on, she said, 'It is not like last time – today we need assistance. It is a very heavy time.'[2] In that moment, we were two mothers sharing stories and a quiet connection, but only one of us lived through the daily ordeal of drought and famine.

I was overwhelmed with aching questions. Sorrow cut deep into my heart over the devastating realities experienced by Felistar and her community. As someone immersed in international justice work, I know how much our world hurts and can be so very broken. What I witnessed with Felistar that day was the very personal reality of our damaged world. Things I knew – but in Kenya knew differently and with profound lament. How could this happen to her? How could this happen to anyone? How could we let this happen to God's world?

I wanted to do something, anything, to help Felistar. I wanted to help the Maasai people stay in their traditional lands and protect their culture from the damage of desperate drifts to the slums of the city. I wanted to help the animals remain wild and survive. I wanted to help restore the parched land overrun by noxious introduced weeds. I could not change the enormity of the situation. But I could do something. I am part of a generation that can do something, and I have a platform, privilege and voice that Felistar and her community still need to have. I offer my best efforts to raise support, unlock resources and get the message out. And I yearn for the Spirit to move with power. I open my hands and pray with purpose.

As we said goodbye, I returned to my four-wheel drive and drove away, leaving behind a cloud of dust.

I wondered what Felistar thought of me or the organisation I worked for.

I considered how long she and her community could live in that harsh landscape.

Was this the destruction of a resilient nomadic people?

Was the climate so damaged that this part of the world would soon become uninhabitable?

I knew I would never forget her face.

O God, will we stop this breakdown of your world?

I ache for justice for Laikipia, for its land and people. I've witnessed extreme poverty over many years and in different locations around the world. It strikes my heart each time while unleashing questions and challenges for myself and the world around me. Meeting Felistar felt different and broke me in new ways. There was something about the enormity of climate change in the drought and famine of Felistar's situation. I found myself mourning for both the present reality and the near future when wild animals and hardy people would no longer be able to exist in those lands.

While you might never travel to remote Kenya, we can connect to this and other stories. If we let ourselves tune in, we know what's going on. We can access the world's news and hear accounts of people responding to poverty or disasters. Like me, you may read reports of future trends for our world, or you may tune in enough to know the direction we're headed in and that we must deal with the causes of these problems.

The oceans rage: James's story

Our next encounter takes us far from the arid dust of Africa to the lapping waters of the blue Pacific Ocean, home to some of our planet's most diverse and stunning ecosystems. From coral reefs teeming with life to volcanic islands rich in culture and history, the Pacific offers a glimpse of paradise to its people. But this paradise is also under threat from the effects of climate change. Rising sea levels, ocean acidification, extreme weather events and biodiversity loss endanger the survival of island nations and the health of our oceans. In this section, we will explore the impacts of climate change on the Pacific region.

James Bhagwan, whom we met earlier, has a rich and complex heritage that spans continents and cultures. His ancestors were forced to leave their homeland in India and worked as enslaved people in the sugar cane fields of Fiji. There, they found a new home among the Fijians, were adopted by the Indigenous community and built relationships. James grew up learning to respect and appreciate the land, waters and people around him. He feels a profound Christian responsibility to protect and care for all creation.

James witnesses rising seas swallowing land, salting soil and destroying freshwater sources and the intricate web of life in the Pacific. He observes how warming waters threaten marine life and, consequently, food security for local communities. Extreme weather events disrupt natural cycles, and intense cyclones devastate homes and infrastructure. Nations such as Kiribati and the Marshall Islands face existential crises as high tides wash over their entire landmass. James emphasises the urgent need for action as Pacific communities battle continual disasters.

Traditional lifestyles based on farming and fishing are being eroded with increasing reliance on imported food, rising costs and urbanisation. James and the Pacific Church support those displaced by climate change, leaving coastal or low-lying islands to relocate to higher ground, understanding the emotional toll of leaving behind sacred places, ancestral graves, cherished memories and cultural identities. He recalls Psalm 137:4, which captures the sorrow of exile: 'How can we sing the songs of the Lord while in a foreign land?'

The tears of exile do not reflect my life experience, and it is a new and sad revelation to hear how powerful this psalm is for grieving Pacific peoples. I can only begin to imagine the grief that our Pacific sisters and brothers are experiencing as they face the loss of their island homes and ancestral lands. I am deeply sorry for the suffering of our Pacific family, and I stand with them in their struggle for justice and survival.

I first met James at the UN Climate Talks during a Pacific-led session on climate refugees. While I was focused on the legal mechanisms to prevent statelessness, James was personally affected by the issue, passionately sharing the voices of his communities facing forced relocation due to climate change. He emphasises,

> You cannot do theology with your backs to the suffering of people. What is our call as the Church to those in pain? We can't just say God is good all the time while they struggle for answers. Our faith and culture provide resilience, even when the land and people are vulnerable.[3]

We can learn a great deal from the faith and resilience of Pacific communities, who view creation as both a sacred gift and a responsibility. Their sense of community allows them to support one another through adversity. In contrast, many Christians in affluent societies have strayed from these core aspects of faith, becoming ensnared by individual consumerism and indifference to broader suffering. It's time to repent and renew our commitment to Jesus, who brings good news to the poor and freedom to the oppressed.

James understands the need to prepare his community for the looming crisis of even more intense climate impacts that threaten lives and livelihoods, viewing it as part of his responsibility as a Methodist pastor and ecumenical leader across Oceania. He profoundly feels the pain of forced migration from island homes that the Bible speaks about of the Israelites in exile in Babylon. He suggests shifting to a new story, drawing on the Bible book of Exodus, which leads out of the land of suffering to a new promised land that God has prepared. James explains what it might mean to hold people and cultures as they transition:

> I liken it to transplanting a tree, where you dig under and around it and put a basket to hold the soil and roots as you transplant it somewhere new. How do we do that in the context of relocation? What is that process of transplanting where you take your soil with you, your identity or culture, and go into a new ground? You are given a certain space

> until your roots can go beyond your own soil into the soil of the land into which you have been transplanted. And for me, those are about the protocols that we need to have with Indigenous communities, how the Church needs to look at these spaces, and how we spiritually address these issues.[4]

Having faced climate impacts for many years, the Pacific Church offers valuable lessons as we prepare for the future. It exemplifies resilience and faithfulness amid adversity, and how to respect creation as a gift and a responsibility from God. The Pacific Church inspires us to speak truth to power and encourage people to seek higher ground, both physically and spiritually. We can apply their example to our own contexts, discovering local ways to be the Church in the world as agents of change and hope.

As we move beyond the Pacific islands and African savannah, we recognise that climate change exacerbates existing threats and creates new challenges. To understand the urgency and complexity, we must listen to those most vulnerable to its impacts.

Cry out: Ray's story

The following account from the climate front lines is from my nation of Australia. Pastor Uncle Ray Minniecon is one of Australia's most respected Aboriginal Christian leaders[5] and a descendant of the Kabi Kabi nation, the Gureng Gureng nation of south-east Queensland, Australia, and the South Sea Islander people. Despite frustration and heartache, he is a gracious, kind, wise man who does not give up actively loving God's world. Ray is called 'Uncle' as a sign of respect as an elder and a remarkable leader, and I am honoured by the wisdom he contributed through his interview.

Uncle Ray's life story is one of resilience and courage in the face of adversity. He ministers amid the trauma of First Nations' 'stolen generations', which was the policy of forcibly removing Aboriginal and Torres Strait Islander children from their families and communities that lasted from the late 1800s to the 1970s.[6]

This policy was part of a broader history of dispossession, discrimination and violence that has inflicted profound suffering on First Nations peoples. Despite apologies and promises, the legacy of this history continues to affect the lives and rights of Indigenous Australians today. The gap between the health, education, employment and justice outcomes of Indigenous and non-Indigenous Australians remains unacceptably wide and slow to close.

Yet Uncle Ray has not given up hope for a better future. He advocates for justice for his people and raises a strong voice for climate action and the role of Indigenous environmental stewardship at national and international levels. He believes that Indigenous peoples have much to offer in the fight for climate justice and that their voices and solutions must be heard and respected. Uncle Ray challenges us to listen, learn and work together as followers of Jesus, and calls us to honour the past, celebrate the present and together shape the future.

Uncle Ray experiences the forefront of the climate crisis and its impact on First Nations peoples. He explains that changes in temperature and rainfall patterns have significant social, health and economic effects:

> The climate crisis has a disproportionate impact on Indigenous peoples because our livelihoods and culture rely on our lands, our waterways, and our oceans for food, medicine and spiritual and cultural practices. Climate impacts are destroying sacred sites for ever with sea level rise and coastal destruction, mining for fossil fuels destroying sites like the ancient Juukan Gorge cave in Western Australia, or gas drilling and fracking that risks the Great Artesian Basin's sole water supply to remote Aboriginal Australians, to cultural practices and ceremonies unable to be performed with extreme desert heat.[7]

Communities relying heavily on the natural environment for their livelihoods are particularly vulnerable. This is true for Indigenous communities living in remote regions, as we have seen with the Pacific communities where James ministers, as well as with Felistar and the Maasai communities. Dr Stella Simiyu, a Kenyan botanist and Christian, agrees:

> The rural poor depend directly on the natural resource base. This is where their pharmacy is, this is where their supermarket is, this is in fact their fuel station, their power company, their water company. What would happen to you if these things were removed from your local neighbourhood?[8]

A multiplying impact of climate damage on First Nations communities is limited access to resources to adapt. As Uncle Ray explains, underlying issues compound this: 'We also face more discrimination, political marginalisation and land disputes. All these things can impede our ability to respond to the climate crisis.'[9] Uncle Ray's outlook is one of lament as he warns us to face current reality:

> On Australia's east coast, we are struggling to repair and restore after devastating floods, with fires shortly before that. The loss and damage have been quite extraordinary just from extreme natural disasters, and when we look at the destruction of our sacred sites, how are we going to mitigate against that because it's already happened?[10]

Uncle Ray's words resonate with me from my experience in international work. I see communities struggle to cope with one disaster after another, with little time to recover or rebuild. My work involves collaborating with local partners around the world to enhance capacity and climate resilience as part of sustainable development. We prioritise disaster preparedness in humanitarian efforts. However, we cannot ignore the harsh reality that resilience has limits, and loss is inevitable for communities facing multiple crises and challenges. And the predictions are grim: this situation will only worsen in the coming years. Uncle Ray laments,

> We're almost at the tipping point, I think. It is very real. In my lifetime, I've seen these changes. This is just in one lifetime, so you can imagine that my children and grandchildren will face more extreme challenges in the future.[11]

There is much wisdom in the care shown by First Nations peoples for the lands, waters and all creation that we can learn from and protect. In Psalm 78:1–3, we are reminded of God's wisdom in hidden things from of old, in things our ancestors have told us that must be passed on to the next generation. Uncle Ray reminds us that Aboriginal Australians have been among the oldest-living continuous cultures for more than sixty thousand years. Studies connect Aboriginal Australians to descendants of people who left Africa and travelled to what has now become the continent of Australia.[12] Archaeological evidence of artefacts confirms the oral history of continuous cultural practices and that people have adapted well to their environment over thousands of years.[13] Uncle Ray's point is one of Aboriginal wisdom and experience: 'We've been stewards of the land, living in harmony with the animals and trees and rivers, the oceans, the stars, and using our traditional knowledge to manage and care for all our natural resources sustainably.'[14]

Now is the time to embrace the invaluable wisdom of Indigenous peoples and those most impacted as we together respond to the challenge of climate change and the collapse of nature. Uncle Ray is part of an international network within the climate and Church movements amplifying First Nations voices:

> We want to ensure our voices and experiences are crucial in shaping global climate policy. We know that Indigenous knowledge systems can help inform climate science and decision-making, and our leaders can provide invaluable insights into the climate crisis's social, economic and cultural dimensions. Our people and communities face incredible, unprecedented challenges and threats to our way of life. And that's not just in Australia; that's all Indigenous peoples globally.[15]

Uncle Ray's voice should influence global climate policy and resonate among us as fellow Christian brothers and sisters. He finds that the wider Church is not listening to the wisdom of Indigenous Christians worldwide and laments 'the way the Bible and its truth has been used as a weapon for advancement and power by the Church, rather than to enhance the whole world that would be beneficial for everybody'.[16] This is a sobering rebuke that expresses a central theme of the problem explored in the previous chapter and the complicity of the Church. Indeed, as God's image-bearers, we have been given tremendous power and must love, not destroy, God's world.

These experiences from Uncle Ray, Reverend James and Felistar are just three examples of a larger crisis. God calls us to be loving and not hard-hearted in the face of what is happening around us (Psalm 95:8). Uncle Ray is urging us to feel and hear these cries, too. To sit and allow ourselves to feel, break and weep as creation groans and our damaging behaviours grieve God. He reminds us that we are not alone in this journey and that God is always with us, even in our pain and suffering. We must act now to make a difference, and do so holding on to the hope for a future where we can live harmoniously with God and all creation.

Engaging with the global Church and seeing ourselves as part of the creation

When we emotionally engage with the cries of our Pacific and Indigenous brothers and sisters, our perspectives are challenged.

In God's wisdom, we are part of a web of relationships and life in a particular place and context. God has created us to live in a mutual relationship with the natural world, and this is something that many First Nations and Global South peoples know well. Might we be caught up in modern, Western thinking that divides humans from nature and people from connections to place? Do we question the Western emphasis on exploiting the earth's resources, or do we limit the sacred and our Church expressions from engaging in broader issues of society and economy?

In a similar way to Uncle Ray, James Bhagwan invites us to open up our vision. He shares a message from his Pacific perspective to the next generation of Christians to heed the 'call to global ecological *metanoia*',[17] a Greek word associated with repentance and change, meaning to let ourselves expand and to convert our thinking. James invites us 'to really reflect on what it means for us to be children of a God who gave his only Son because he loved the whole world'.[18] We are not one-dimensional beings but are relationally physical, spiritual and emotional. We are complex and have relationships as part of the mystical body of Christ and in our physical locality. James urges,

> In loving and serving God, we are called to honour all those relationships. Is it possible for us to see creation as our brother and sister? Or, if not, can we then look at creation as our neighbour? And what does it mean to love our neighbour in the sense of what we are going through at this time? What does it mean to be a good steward?[19]

Like many Pacific and Indigenous communities, James uses relational and familial language to describe God's interconnected creation.[20] It is worth acknowledging that this may feel uncomfortable or challenging for some people from Western-thinking contexts. Yet the insights gained from Christians through diverse cultural lenses are of immense value and are perspectives that must be heard. A long tradition of some of the Church's greatest thinkers reminds the West in particular that it is not the centre of the world and has lost its connections to place, people and embodiment. A mindset shift is needed to heed this call. Theologian Lesslie Newbigin made this point in the 1970s as a returning missionary from India to the UK when he argued for the richness of reading the Bible in dialogue with people from other cultures.[21] Jocabed Solano, an Indigenous Guna theologian from Panama involved in the Lausanne and Langham Christian movements, highlights the importance of all relationships:

> Indigenous perspectives can help us recover the deeply biblical connections between people, land and faith which we see in Scripture. Indigenous peoples also offer a way for the Euro-centric church to return to a theology and mission based on particular relationships to a particular space, which helps us see how our theology does have an impact on the earth.[22]

These perspectives urge a more holistic and interconnected view of creation, reminding us that our faith and actions are deeply intertwined with the well-being of the earth. By listening to and learning from Indigenous voices, we can enrich our understanding and practice of faith in ways that honour God's creation and our place within it.

The Bible uses relational and surprisingly anthropomorphic language to speak of the earth, such as the trees rejoicing (Psalm 96:12); creatures, ecosystems and humans together praising God (Psalm 148); the land weeping (Job 31:38); the rocks crying out (Luke 19:40); or creation groaning (Romans 8:22). As we have learned, this is not saying that the earth is a living person, or that created things are divine or to be worshipped in themselves (Romans 1:25), but rather that God has created us and the natural world to live in a close mutual relationship.[23] There is a long Christian history of such language and recognition of our relatedness in God's created order rather than separation from the world where we live and on which we depend. Francis of Assisi, the brown-robed Italian friar who famously loved animals, spoke about Brother Sun or Sister Moon. John Stott spoke of learning from birds, creatures and the works of God in nature, recognising that we are part of the created order ourselves, with care for creation and responding to the current ecological crisis a necessary mark of discipleship and involvement in God's mission.[24] So, too, do Indigenous viewpoints see us as part of a web of interconnected relationships and bring a deep connection to their natural world.

In this chapter, we have heard global perspectives and accounts from the front lines of climate impacts. We have had the opportunity to be shaped by people from diverse cultures and tasked with respecting our sacred connection with creation and our role as caretakers of the earth. Let's rethink our place in creation, and take forward a renewed sense of purpose and a broader perspective from the wisdom and courage encountered through these pages.

Reflection

Sit in prayer and invite God to soften your heart.

What new insights and understanding did you gain from listening to global perspectives?

How might you respond with empathy and action that reflects Christ's love and justice?

In what ways can you rediscover the deep connection with and stewardship of creation seen in communities like those in the Pacific?

Commit your reflections and responses regarding the climate crisis to prayer.

Join with the community of believers and pray as our Saviour taught us:[25]

Our Father in heaven,
hallowed be your name,
your kingdom come,
your will be done,
on earth as in heaven.
Give us today our daily bread.
Forgive our sins
as we forgive those who sin against us.
Lead us not into temptation
but deliver us from evil.
For the kingdom, the power,
and the glory are yours,
now and for ever.
Amen.

Part 3

5

Call: tuning into our own calling

And what does the LORD require of you?
To act justly and to love mercy
and to walk humbly with your God.
(Micah 6:8)

Discovering our calling enables us to engage with God's plan and the part we might play. In this chapter, I will share some stories that have shaped how I found my calling to care for people on the margins and my awakening to responsibility for God's creation. I will also highlight stories of calling to care for the environment from our contributors, revealing how God has shaped their paths. I hope that by my sharing these experiences, you will reflect on your own journey and consider how God may be inviting you to participate in his mission of love and justice.

How I found my calling to care: Jo's story

When I reflect on the first season of my story, I feel a deep sense of gratitude for the faith I developed as a deep-feeling kid, which helped me cultivate a strong sense of compassion. This compassion was shaped by the love shown by my parents and my frail Nanna, especially in relation to my aunt Rae, who had Down's syndrome.

I was a bright and earnest young girl from a suburban Christian family, the youngest of three sisters. One of my happiest childhood memories is of visiting Nanna and Aunt Rae in a country town called Echuca. I loved those visits. I cherished the deep connection my mum's family had to that place and how right it felt to be there together.

My sisters and I would pick roses and daisies, jump over the sprinkler watering the lawn and breathe in the fresh air. Echuca, situated on Australia's mighty Murray River, was surrounded by farmland and abundant eucalyptus trees. The expansive landscape left a lasting impression on me. It was a place filled with love and joy.

But then everything changed. Rae had a severe stroke and went into a frozen state, robbed of her body and speech. Soon, my Nanna also deteriorated: both needed care in a nursing home. Nanna lived for only a few more months. We faithfully visited my aunt until she, too, passed away. I was devastated. This was my first chasm of grief as I lost two family members who had brought loving solidness and knitted me to the place that made me happy.

Because of that, as a pain-filled girl, I turned inward and found a friend in Jesus. I was confused and traumatised by death and loss. We no longer visited Echuca; we no longer had our loved ones in the rhythm of our lives. The brokenness of the world hurts. I can now appreciate that this time developed my faith that grew roots like Echuca's eucalyptus trees that are exposed and searching for water by the river. In my pain and loneliness, I felt a growing concern for people on the margins like Rae. I clung to the verse, 'Come near to God and he will come near to you' (James 4:8). I didn't know there was much more to discover about God's compassion and justice at that time.

In the years following, God revealed to me his heart for marginalised people, for people in poverty and for justice. I am grateful to the East Timorese refugees who arrived at my youth group and opened my eyes to God's concern for the oppressed, which is evident throughout the Bible. Over time, this expanded as I grasped that making things right was part of the vision of the kingdom of God. This evolved into a personal calling for me to be his hands and feet.

I studied law and international politics at university, seeking to understand and change the systems that create inequality. But it was not until I went to India as a volunteer to learn about faith-led community development and holistic mission that I saw the face of poverty and a new dimension to the power of God's love. I met people who lived in villages who had nothing but their dignity. I also met Indian Christians serving them with compassion and integrity, showing me what being part of God's kingdom means.

That experience changed me. I returned home with a fire in my heart and helped start a youth movement fighting poverty and promoting education and empowerment. We called ourselves Oaktree and grew from a small team to a large organisation, working with peers in the Global South, fundraising, organising concerts and rallies, and campaigning to increase foreign aid. We were young, but we were bold and passionate. We believed we could change the world.

I worked as a lawyer for refugees, challenging unfair laws and representing my clients' hopes and fears amid considerable stress. I saw my clients' pain and resilience and the limits of the legal system, which needed extensive changes. Then, one day, I had the most significant legal victory of my working life when I won an influential case in the High Court of Australia for my Cambodian client. But yet I felt a sense of conflict, knowing he still faced a long, uncertain road ahead. I looked up from the court building in my nation's capital to the Parliament House perched on the hill, where the laws and decisions began. I felt a pull, a curiosity, a desire. I had been there briefly before, speaking to politicians, and had seen the potential for making a difference at the source of power. I wondered if God was calling me to something new. I didn't know then what the next part of my story would be: that God would lead me into a broader role that would equip people of faith in advocacy and care for our planet. My focus at that point was solely on people. We don't always understand what God is doing in our lives until later.

> We know that the whole creation has been groaning in labour pains until now; and not only the creation, but we ourselves, who have the first fruits of the Spirit, groan inwardly while we wait.
> (Romans 8:22–23, NRSVA)

My awakening to the groans of creation came like labour pains when I became a mother. The sheer physicality and pain of giving birth was for me a thing of overwhelming awe. Becoming a mother became my stripping back of layers and baring of my innermost being, with growth and challenge beyond what I could have imagined. I was operating out of my comfort zone and away for a time from the consuming flow of my outward justice vocation. I realised I was a caring lioness with protective fears of catastrophe for my precious little boys, for, by then, there were two. And in that season, I changed. The depths of love I felt for my little boys were beyond what I could have imagined, and the ministry of cuddles and wonder was a balm to my soul. I came to know more of myself and had time to know God more deeply and personally as I encountered vulnerability and loss of control in the world of young children.

When I would get a moment, I would locate myself in nature to connect, and I came to appreciate my relationship with God in creation in new and profound ways. I learned to listen, be still in nature and appreciate God as the Creator holding all things. I'd grown up loving the wilds of nature, dimly aware among the noise of being an adult how nature revealed so much about God and was so good for my soul. Away from the daily grind of an office job, I could marvel at the depths of Creator God, that 'The earth is the LORD's and all that is in it' (Psalm 24:1, NRSVA).

As I walked my little boys along bush paths beside my local river, I thought a lot about the future of our planet for them and what it meant to love this generation and future generations. I grew a stronger sense of the Father's love for all his creation, just as I was filled with love for my little boys and was trying to care for the world around them now and into the future. Caring for creation became personal and went from my head to my heart. I took steps beyond the simple living I had sought over the years into more intentional care for our planet. I used cloth nappies. We ate less meat. I caught the bus. We lived off less. I came to appreciate all the home-cooked meals and simple old-fashioned ways my parents had taught me.

God used this time of my life to point me beyond my focus on justice for human beings to grasp his broader plans for restoring and renewing all things. As I grasped more of God's story, I grew in my theological understanding and conviction around creation justice, the urgency for climate action and my whole-of-life calling personally and to the Church.

I began working at Tearfund Australia, a Christian international development and advocacy agency that has been part of my life since my teenage years and my time in India. God provided me with opportunities to grow in public engagement and leadership, focusing on advocacy and climate justice. I trained Christian groups, engaged with politicians, and had the privilege to be a co-creator of the Renew Our World campaign for the international Church, which was outlined earlier in this book.

I realised the importance of climate justice and how it related to my calling. I was disheartened by the Global North's contribution to extreme poverty and climate change yet my country's political turmoil that hindered progress. While the Church in my country seemed absent, I found hope in the active pursuit of justice by the Church in the Global South. Motivated by this, I committed to making a difference and inviting fellow followers of Jesus to join the cause.

This journey has been challenging and has its tensions. For example, as a busy mother of young children navigating a high-consumer culture and also balancing work outside the home, I, too, often make unconsidered, convenient choices that opt for quick solutions that do not reflect care for our planet. Despite many failings, I continue to take steps, knowing that God has been influencing every aspect of my life.

***

This journey of discovering a calling to care reminds us that our own stories are often shaped by the people and experiences around us. Just as my compassion for others and the natural world grew from personal experiences and faith, we, too, can trace our shaping and calling in our lives.

What about you? Perhaps there are things in your story that drew you to explore the topics of this book. There may be something in your past, present or yearnings for the future that comes to mind. Consider how God has been tracing his story through yours.

Think about the moments that have touched your heart and the people who have influenced your perspective. Significant people might come to mind, or moments where you could not ignore the impact of human actions or something about the natural world. These experiences can guide us to a deeper understanding of why we care and what we might do next to serve and express our values throughout our lives. It helps us see how interconnected our lives are with the world around us, and that each of us has a unique part to play. We will move next to explore the callings to care of some of the contributors interviewed, and this presents an opportunity to follow something in their example or translate aspects into the discovery of your own calling. As you ponder these things, join in this simple but profound prayer taken from Pete Greig and the 24-7 Prayer movement:[1]

May God's image in me be restored,
and my imagination in God be re-storied.
Amen.

God's call changing lives: stories of creation care leaders

The following personal stories of conviction regarding creation justice and awakening to God's plan enrich our understanding of diverse faith journeys and the expanding scope of the gospel. These accounts from our interviewed contributors provide different insights into discipleship responses and allow us to reflect on God's creation call in our own lives.

The awakening of a movement: Tony's story

Throughout Christian history, every so often, God has raised up unexpected leaders to bring global change. One of the most startling examples of this in the creation justice space is the Australian agronomist and missionary Tony Rinaudo. Known as the 'forest maker', he has transformed millions of lives and hectares of land by pioneering the revolutionary technique we heard about earlier, unlocking the hidden potential of dry and barren lands to grow millions of trees. His work and story have been amplified through *The Forest Maker* film, his celebrated memoir *The Forest Underground* and various media outlets.[2] He would never say this himself, but Tony is a big deal. He has received the Right Livelihood Award (the Alternative Nobel Prize) for contributing to humanity and the environment. Sharing his story is crucial to spreading the movement and the restoration hope he brings.

I had the privilege of hosting Tony and his wife, Liz, in my home, sipping tea and listening to his fantastic story. He wore his characteristic blue shirt and spoke with his gentle Italian-Australian country manner, radiating humility, passion and dedication. Tony's faith motivates him. He is a disciple of Jesus, persevering to make a difference. I find Tony's story inspiring, with crucial lessons to learn.

As a boy, three convictions set Tony on his path. The first was his despair at the environmental destruction he witnessed growing up in the countryside, seeing clear felling of the Australian bush and the erosion and loss of biodiversity that followed. Second, he became angry about the links between environmental damage and global poverty. He felt powerless that in his valley, farmers grew tobacco, yet fellow children born elsewhere went to bed hungry. The third conviction was his mother's strong faith, which he took on for himself. With a childlike innocence, he asked God to simply use him somehow and somewhere to make a difference. Since then, he has tried to stay true to that prayer. God had placed a calling on his heart. He had a desire for justice and wanted to make things right.[3]

In the early 1980s, Tony, Liz and their baby son moved to Niger. The following years were a struggle. A devastating famine set in, and his attempts at tree planting failed. At that time Niger experienced severe drought, strong winds that buried and sandblasted crops, and hot, arid soil. The soil was bare of nutrients, and the water table dropped, resulting in women spending long hours trying to find water. It was an incredibly challenging context in which to choose to live, work and raise a young family.

One day, during a quiet time, Tony read of God's power in our world from Psalm 104:30:

> When you send your Spirit,
> they are created,
> and you renew the face of the ground.

He felt this was significant and he should reflect on it, but he quickly rushed off to the call of the day's work. That day, as he let down the air in the vehicle's tyres in the middle of a lunar landscape with soil that looked beyond repair, Tony had his eureka moment and saw a tiny bush pushing through a crack in the ground. It was a leaf signature revealing that it was not bush but, in fact, came from a tree. At that moment, Tony remembered the psalm and a great weight was lifted from his shoulders. God was working through Tony and awakening the forest underground.

Tony suddenly realised that if living tree roots were under the ground and naturally trying to grow, with simple pruning and careful management the trees could grow beyond small bushes. There was already a forest underground! His hypothesis worked, and soon he convinced other local farmers how to do what became globally known as FMNR (Farmer Managed Natural Regeneration). This was done with minimal cost, maximum sustainability and remarkable scalability.

Tony Rinaudo firmly believes that the individual actions of ordinary people matter. He reminds us to take steps, learn from our mistakes, improve our knowledge and competence, and gain confidence over time to achieve something. Tony drew on Ephesians 2:10, knowing that God had things in hand and had prepared good things for him to do, and this kept him grounded even in setbacks. He cites the importance of finding like-minded people on the journey to be encouraged by and to encourage them.

Tony also agrees that when we take action, we influence others, and sometimes those others may be too timid to start on their own but may mimic us. When enough people do this, we see an ecosystem of growth, and the impact of many people doing small things is vast.

Tony actively encourages younger generations and passes on the hope he has found. He sees his younger self reflected in the passion and cynicism of young people who feel disheartened by the complexity of the challenges ahead or the sentiment that it's too late. He encourages people to believe in themselves and the gifts God has given them, trusting that God is on our side as we yearn for a safe climate and healthy functioning environment.

Tony reminds us to start small, do what we can and go as far as we can see, and that we will always be able to see further when we get there. Tony's reflection rings true: our vantage point changes when we've taken steps and move further on a journey, trusting God with the results. And responding to climate change is indeed a journey; as leading climate scientist Tamsin Edwards acknowledges, we are all both heroes and villains:

> Climate change is not something that is simply won or lost. It is a curve that we can keep bending towards a better world. The future is looking better than we imagined, but it is not yet as good as we hope. What happens next is up to us. Future generations will know how we did.[4]

Creation's call: Ruth's story

Dr Ruth Valerio is an environmentalist, theologian and social activist dedicated to inspiring a whole-life response to environmental breakdown and poverty. It was Ruth's theological framework that guided us earlier. Ruth has authored several impactful books that intertwine faith, environmentalism and social justice. Some of her works include *Saying Yes to Life*,[5] published as the Archbishop of Canterbury's Lent book for 2020, and her practical guide *L Is for Lifestyle: Christian living that doesn't cost the earth*.[6] How did Ruth's journey begin? What sparked her passion for creation and conviction regarding environmental stewardship?

Ruth Valerio's life took a turn when she borrowed a little book from a friend. The book was Chris Seaton's *Whose Earth?*[7] The timing was right after the 1992 UN Rio Earth Summit when world leaders gathered to discuss the environmental crisis. The book explored how the Bible and ecological care are connected. Ruth was amazed by this new angle on what seemed a strange question. She was a young adult studying theology at university but had not realised that the Bible is about the entire world, not just people. She says, 'It was like the scales fell from my eyes. And I just saw an aspect of my Christian faith that had been missing.'[8] That little book sparked Ruth's passion, which has continued for thirty years. Ruth wanted to learn more about how the Bible speaks to the problems faced by our world and care for our environment. She understood that it really matters as a follower of Jesus to be concerned and involved in what's happening in the world. In the intervening years, Ruth has seen a shift whereby environmental and human development organisations have aligned. She explains,

> In our increasingly globalised world, and with the big global issues that we are facing, we now know that you can't tackle the environment without thinking about poverty and wealth; they both contribute to our environmental issues. You can't care for people without thinking about the lands they live on, the air they breathe and the seas they fish in. And you can't think about the natural world without thinking about the people who live there and who impact it in different ways.[9]

'You can't care for people without thinking about the lands they live on, the air they breathe and the seas they fish in. And you can't think about the natural world without thinking about the people who live there and who impact it in different ways.'
(Ruth Valerio)

Ruth's working life set out with the conservation charity A Rocha – we heard earlier about her development there of the immensely successful Eco Church scheme. She then brought together environmental and poverty work, leading global advocacy at Tearfund and subsequently with the organisation Embrace the Middle East. Ruth is often sought out for her public commentary on various media or speaking platforms. She is a role model in living out her faith sustainably and inspires others to do the same. Ruth is known for her generosity and encouragement, and her warm smile brightens any room she enters. I am grateful for her wisdom and guidance as my mentor, fellow believer and contributor to this book. As I have followed God's calling, having mentors like Ruth has been significant.

Mentors have also played a significant role in Kuki Rokhum's journey.

Shaping and guided growth: Kuki's story

Kuki Rokhum, whom we heard from earlier, has a faith story that is a testament to the quiet strength that grows through one's heritage and convictions. One singular, defining revelation doesn't mark her story; instead, it's shaped by mentors and the rich traditions of her tribal and Christian upbringing from her family's origins in Mizoram, India. Kuki's father profoundly influenced her view of God's creation. He never preached about caring for nature; instead, he lived it. Whether it was a tree, an insect or an animal, he showed kindness and respect. Kuki remembers him gently stopping her from harming a bug, saying, 'No, we shouldn't hurt it.' His actions instilled in Kuki a deep respect for all living things and the belief that every part of creation deserves care. While Kuki learned in Sunday school how God created his world and made everything beautiful, as a child she never linked it to her attitude towards the rest of creation. That came from her father and family.[10]

As a young adult, Kuki was influenced by individuals who demonstrated integrity in their everyday life choices, much like her father. She engaged in discussions with them about these decisions.

Pivotal moments shaped Kuki's understanding of ecological stewardship and compassion for those in need around a kitchen table in London, where she lived for a time with Dave and Anne Bookless. Additionally, the guidance from C. B. Samuel directed her towards a career path she hadn't initially envisioned.

Over the next two decades, Kuki served at EFICOR (Evangelical Fellowship of India Commission on Relief), witnessing the impact of ecological crises on impoverished communities across India. She reflects with gratitude on the mentors and influencers who have shaped her journey and sees God's hand in it all. Kuki appreciates the sense of a journey that involves learning, making mistakes, falling off track and finding a way back. Influencers have played a crucial role in this process.

She recalls moments when others offered her valuable advice or encouragement at critical times, such as a mentor who advised her to use any platform well if she ever received one. For Kuki, this has included public speaking, leadership roles and the ability to influence. These experiences resonated with her, and she implemented the lessons learned, even when she felt terrified or confused about why God opened up certain opportunities for her.

Kuki knows the importance of passing on guidance and influence. She urges, 'It's so important for us as more mature Christians or people who lead in influential positions to use the discernment, wisdom and experience God has given us to influence younger people to speak into those moments.'[11] Kuki seeks to do this with integrity as she plays a part in building the creation care movement and be the person who walks the talk with integrity in everyday life. She reflects, 'You just build it up, layer by layer – those influences, conversations and encounters you have with people. I think it all adds up and makes you into who you are becoming in this journey.' Kuki encourages that, rather than this being a lonely journey, a growing body of people is realising that others are also trying to make a difference and are part of groups and movements for change together.

Kuki firmly believes personal choices are significant for collective influence. Initially sceptical, Kuki once dismissed small gestures, such as purchasing fair-trade coffee or recycling, as mere tokenism. However, an incident involving a persistently dripping tap at her home in Delhi served as an epiphany. She was astonished at how swiftly a bucket placed beneath the drip filled overnight. Kuki hadn't anticipated the bucket filling so rapidly or the roof tank emptying, and as she realised the waste and cumulative loss, so, too, did she understand the truth that every action counts, no matter how small.[12]

Kuki regularly encounters people who feel daunted by the sheer scale of the issues we face, where the apparent solutions seem to lie in sweeping policy reforms or tackling corporate giants. We may feel voiceless in such scenarios. Nevertheless, the accumulation of contributions builds impact. Kuki advocates doing our utmost, regardless of where we are. Our small purchasing steps send a message and can influence consumption markets, and our modest acts, such as writing a letter to a decision-maker, do matter. Kuki encourages,

> Whether our conscientiousness, informed consumption choices, or restraint, these steps matter and help alleviate strain on our planet. And when many of us make similar choices, it amplifies the effect, steering us towards a more just world and a healthier environment.[13]

Do the best you can, wherever you are. The United Nations has even embraced this concept, launching a global 'Be the Change' initiative.[14] While your actions and decisions may seem unconventional to others, they will be remembered. You will make a difference, and your sphere of influence is poised to expand as you persist in taking steps forward. Kuki's journey began not with the grand declarations on public stages that she delivers today, but with embracing small moments and actions, which gradually gained momentum.[15] Similarly, Tony Rinaudo was once labelled the 'eccentric white farmer' for his unconventional approach,[16] yet saw his influence and impact grow through steadfast perseverance.

A rubbish moment: Dave's story

God's awakening of Dave Bookless to care for creation took a different path. Dave's passion for stewarding God's creation started more than thirty years ago. The moment came for him at the end of a holiday with his wife, Anne, on a small, beautiful island with wildlife and sandy beaches. It was the late 1980s, and the island had no waste collection. At the end of a fortnight's holiday, Dave was told to take their rubbish to the end of a little path and deal with it. What had once been a beach had become the island rubbish tip. In the act of throwing away his rubbish, Dave had a profound but powerful sense of God speaking in his mind and heart, saying, 'How do you think I feel about what you're doing to my world?'[17] That question unlocked a whole lot of other questions about lifestyle and environmental problems. Suddenly, Dave realised that God cared about all of that and didn't care only about people, and certainly not only about souls. Dave had grown up in a solid Christian context, as the son of missionaries in India, and was studying for ordination. Dave describes his early faith as a classic but somewhat limited and individualistic evangelical understanding, focusing on a gospel that was about him and Jesus, his soul being saved, going to heaven and sharing the good news of Jesus' forgiveness with others. After Dave's 'rubbish moment' on the island, his faith was challenged, expanded, and engaged with significant issues facing the world. As he continued to study theology, he reread his Bible with 'new glasses'.[18] Previously, Dave had read the Bible with lenses simply about God and people, but suddenly he was looking at what the Bible says about God and all of creation. This ultimately led to his doctorate on the Bible and wildlife conservation. Dave's story is more fully explored in his well-known book *God Doesn't Do Waste.*[19]

***

This collection of stories highlights transformative moments, including Dave's life-changing experience, Kuki's father's kindness and Ruth's inspiration from a book. Each account reflects God's calling and emphasises the importance of caring for creation.

God has intertwined the stories of our contributors in surprising and meaningful ways. For example, Kuki is the godmother of Dave's daughter, and Tony has worked alongside Kuki in the past. Ruth, Dave and Katharine have collaborated on various initiatives and have spoken at shared events. C. B. Samuel has mentored Kuki, while James and Uncle Ray met while advocating for justice on a global scale. These examples illustrate the diverse relationships that embody the growing Christian movement and serve as vibrant holistic signs of the kingdom. Ruth Padilla DeBorst encourages us to 'allow God's Spirit to weave us into God's community of intertwined roots of radical discipleship, as citizens of God's kingdom and promoters of just conviviality'.[20]

These narratives are not mere stories to read and forget; they are invitations to reflect on our faith and discipleship. Take a moment to consider what aspects of the stories resonated with you, and the significant individuals or ideas that have shaped how you interact with the world. Think about what brings you joy, and how that aligns with God's guidance and the good works prepared for you (Ephesians 2:10).

It is essential to remember that the Lord does not require specific types of service, such as charity work, science or public speaking. Rather, he asks us to act justly, to love mercy and to walk humbly with him (Micah 6:8).

The woven stories of our contributors and their commitments to a sustainable future help us identify ways to follow, and we can translate their examples into our own actions. Together, the Church fosters collective efforts for good as we work towards hopeful change and momentum for a safer climate future.

Reflection

Pause.

Consider the storylines of your life and shaping.

Ask God what aspects of your life will be recalled today in the quietness.

To help discover your call and carry you forward in response, imagine Jesus looking at you, with his power and love. This is the same Jesus who washed the feet of his disciples and willingly died on the cross. Look at him looking at you, and allow yourself to notice the love and humility in how he looks at you. This is a spiritual exercise of Saint Teresa of Ávila, drawn from Anthony de Mello's *Sadhana: A Way to God.*[21]

So take a moment to find a comfortable space, quiet yourself and slow your breathing as you invite contemplation and an encounter with Jesus with this prayerful exercise.

> Imagine you see Jesus standing before you … He is looking at you … Notice him looking at you …
>
> Notice him looking at you … *lovingly and humbly.*[22]

When you are ready, write or draw your storylines of what makes you and how God has lovingly shaped you.

Do you have a sense of your response as a disciple of Jesus?

Is there a specific area of concern you're passionate about?

How might that connect to something in your story?

Perhaps you notice a prompting or alignment with your gifts?

Take some time to explore it further!

Lord Jesus,
I pause in your presence, seeking your guidance and love.
Help me reflect on my life and see how you have shaped me.
As I respond to the call of creation justice, may your powerful love carry me forward.
Let me see you looking at me with love and humility, filling me with peace.
Guide me as I recognise my gifts and passions, and strengthen my resolve to contribute to your call.
Amen.

6

Response: being part of something bigger

> God has made us new creations, so that our heart is being renewed to want the same thing. It's not me versus God, but it's me and God versus the power of sin in the flesh.
> (Katharine Hayhoe)[1]

Spiritual sickness and extractive mindsets have brought humanity to the brink of ecological disaster. However, our urgent and hopeful responses demonstrate the resilience of the human spirit. There is hope in addressing climate change *if* we take action. We do not act alone; we are supported by the collective strength of a community that encourages one another, and by the power of the Spirit. As God works in our world and through the Church, a movement emerges that renews and spreads goodness. Let's explore how we can pray boldly and take meaningful action to make a difference.

Our climate response is holistic, taking place through every aspect of our lives. While we reduce the environmental impact of our lifestyles, the larger challenge lies with the extensive actions of corporations and governments, which bear a greater responsibility. We can become a powerful force for change when we all take sustainable steps and urge industries and governments to respond with urgency. Planning these actions starts within our own sphere of influence and expands to create a wider impact. This approach contributes to the momentum for transformation in response to climate change. When we put our God-given passions into practice and seek guidance and collaboration with others, we rise to meet our generation's defining challenge.

How we will achieve transformational change

The monumental challenge of climate change necessitates systemic transformations that far exceed minor adjustments. As we have heard, we need transformation across all parts of our systems, and influential decision-makers in government and business are vital. Let's overview the required systemic changes and then consider the role of individual actions in making a difference.

Three major things need to occur to begin to heal our earth.

First, we must do all in our power to responsibly, immediately and urgently cease the activities and harmful habits that worsen our earth's health and pump greenhouse gas emissions into the air.[2] Every fraction of a degree of global heating that can be avoided will reduce devastating impacts. We are beyond the point where certain changes to our earth's health are irreversible. The more we reduce emissions now, the more possible it will be to adapt to unavoidable changes.

Second, we need to remove excess carbon in our atmosphere as it can continue to fuel climate change well into the future; and we need to draw it down as quickly, safely and fairly as possible. Carbon drawdown can come from nature-based solutions on land, including ecosystem renewal, reafforestation and agriculture changes, ocean and coastal ecosystem care, as well as technological innovations.[3] As James Bhagwan said, our earth's lungs are powered by the trees and the seas.[4]

The third fundamental way to heal is to adapt to ongoing changes and build resilience for the future. We must adjust our ways of life and systems to try to live with the climate damage already set in motion.

These three areas address our earth's climate symptoms and underlying causes.

With these significant transformations needed, do our individual efforts truly contribute to meaningful change? The answer is a resounding *yes.* It is imperative for individuals to actively engage in shaping the change we wish to see in the world across a range of influences – from prayerful advocacy to voting, mindful consumption and lifestyle choices. These personal actions are integral to driving essential systemic shifts propelled by the collective force of the people. Katharine Hayhoe urges that systemic transformation happens with every action:

> Climate action can be taken at every level, in every city, in every school, in every place of work and every neighborhood and every home. How we catalyze that change is by using our voice. The biggest way that we can affect people is through our climate shadow. And that means that everything we do matters.[5]

It is vital to spread the word about climate action in your networks, to talk about it, and to speak up to those in power as a politically active global citizen. In her book *Saving Us*, Katharine Hayhoe explores the concept of our 'climate shadows' of influence. She highlights the power we all have through communicating our actions on climate change with people in our networks, such as solutions we are putting into practice or things that personally motivate and matter to us. Our lifestyle choices and community actions can influence larger systemic changes and, with intention, can amplify our impact through collective efforts.

Raise a powerful voice

Consider how you can use your voice to influence all sorts of decision-makers as you seek sustainable approaches. There may be limitations within your context where advocacy may not be safe or possible, but there will also be opportunities for influence. You don't need to be partisan to the left or the right but you can speak out of love for people and places. You may be surprised at how much influence you can have and the momentum that builds as you take many steps for change. Some of these decision-makers will be political with the power to change large-scale policies. For instance, the vaccine equity campaign of the Micah coalition during the pandemic underscored the importance of global solidarity, with significant wins from the Australian government that ensured fairer access to life-saving vaccines in the Asia–Pacific region. Look for ways to unite and carry out your collective influence.

For those in the context of a democracy, defend it and use it to amplify the voices on the front lines. This can look like engaging with petitions, handwritten letters, lobbying, training local groups or prayer vigils, non-violent direct action, social or earned media engagement, getting behind lawyers to engage in test cases in the courts, and many other tactics that might be relevant at a given time. As we lobby decision-makers to make large-scale institutional, policy or corporate changes, it is helpful to show how we care personally and have taken ethical steps in our own sphere of influence, too.

Momentum for social change

The essence of transformative movements lies in taking action and uniting with others who share our vision for a better world. Through small, consistent efforts, each of us contributes to the momentum needed to overcome the steep challenge of climate change. Katharine Hayhoe is optimistic about the combined strength of our collective action and that we are moving fast towards a sustainable future that is not only possible but already underway.[6] The genuine prospect for change is quantified by Erica Chenoweth, a Harvard political scientist specialising in people power, who implores,

> We must not succumb to the belief that our actions don't matter and that we have no power. In many countries around the world, a 3.5 per cent tipping point has led to major breakthroughs for protest movements. And studies suggest that there is a 25 per cent tipping point for genuine behavioural change and transformation on a larger scale. Both of these tipping points are within reach. Tens of millions of people have been taking action to transform our relationship to the planet. Formidable obstacles remain, but if we take history as

> our guide, these can be overcome by good strategy, effective organizing, and people power.[7]

Social change is within our grasp! Think about the transformational experience of women's empowerment in only a few generations. Recall how the transatlantic slave trade was deeply rooted in many societies and economies, but significant change was achievable. Remember how, in the recent past, colonial occupation, racial segregation and denial of civil rights or the rule of dictators used to dominate numerous countries. Think in your local context of how decision-makers have been held accountable, or where something that felt impossible has shifted in social attitudes. Throughout history, people have shifted their mindsets and exerted pressure on decision-makers, bringing previously unimaginable change.

So begin change within your sphere of influence. Take your everyday acts of how you live, vote, give financially, speak up and pray as an act of worship and response to God's call. Remember that consumer choices influence business decisions, and ordinary voters affect the outcome of democratic elections, giving political permission or cover for how governments operate in our community. Look for ways to come together with others, support one another and seek maximum impact.

Make a plan for just and sustainable changes in your everyday life

As we seek systemic change for climate justice, let's commit to being responsible stewards in key areas of our lives, such as sustainable food choices, plastic waste reduction, cleaner energy and transport, and mindful consumption. It's crucial to recognise that these choices depend on individual circumstances and resources; not everyone can afford or make significant changes.

We should avoid setting unattainable standards and understand that we may stumble along the way. Still, we can take meaningful steps within our means, like the faithful widow (Mark 12:42–44) who offered two small coins. You will find plenty of information in your context about what you could do, and this section of the book provides a resource with space for you to plan your action as you clarify your response.

> Where might God be nudging and challenging you as you examine your lifestyle? What are you going to do about it? Changing your everyday life choices begins today, tomorrow, next week and the following weeks. Put your God-given insight into practice.
>
> Write a letter to yourself about the changes you want to make in your day-to-day life as a promise for the future. Then plan some practical steps you can take in the short term. What do you want to report to yourself in a month or two? What do you want to say to God?

We are warned in James 1:22–25 not to squander our God-given insight foolishly but instead put it into practice:

> Do not merely listen to the word, and so deceive yourselves. Do what it says. Anyone who listens to the word but does not do what it says is like someone who looks at his face in a mirror and, after looking at himself, goes away and immediately forgets what he looks like. But whoever looks intently into the perfect law that gives freedom and continues in it – not forgetting what they have heard but doing it – they will be blessed in what they do.

What are some practical lifestyle steps to minimise harm and maximise good in your context? The following suggestions touch on some domains of life for you to consider and apply to your circumstances, and there is a list of resources for further exploration at the end of the book.

- I encourage you to begin with an exploration of *sustainable and ethical food choices*. Reducing meat and dairy consumption impacts carbon emissions and is a significant step in a more sustainable food system. Much has been written on the future of food for both high-consumer contexts and smallholder farmers in poverty, but this overview is brief. For example, you could begin with meat-free Mondays, three fewer items of packaged foods weekly, seasonal local produce and eating leftovers.

Try growing some things in a garden or pots. You might be ready for more significant steps concerning food, and I encourage you to explore new and local opportunities.

- The next domains of faithfulness through lifestyle change to consider are *energy use and transport*. Each country is different regarding the transition to renewables, but I encourage you to look for ways to reduce your energy use and, where possible, to transition to clean, renewable energy sources. The environmental footprint of our buildings, whether our homes or local churches, can be within our influence to change. For a nation such as mine with vast sunshine, the uptake of solar panels in homes is widespread and cost effective. When we shift our mindsets to conserve energy use, we turn off lights or reduce our reliance on energy for heating or cooling.

  This mindset transformation considers the impact of extractive energy and waste from the production of consumables, from fashion to other lifestyle areas. When considering transport options, whether a vehicle, public transport or something else, opt for electric, hybrid or low-carbon transport alternatives where possible. Eco-friendly transport differs by context, availability and circumstances, such as whether we need to travel for work, and commute in sprawling suburbs or remote towns, and whether public transport, safe biking or other alternatives are possible. Despite differences across contexts, we can take steps to seek eco-friendly transport in our lives and speak up for policy change to make alternatives possible.
- The area of *plastic pollution* and its environmental and climate damage is a fast-growing problem. Plastic production and supposed disposal have a significant carbon footprint, not to mention harm in some of the most marginalised places that lack waste systems. Look for ways to eliminate single-use

plastic, especially during shopping and at home. Like any change, begin with manageable steps and go from there. In my busy household, we struggle with plastic packaging as we succumb to what's convenient, but we are trying to tackle this one room at a time. For example, in the bathroom and in our context, this means solid shampoo bars, old-fashioned soap in waste-free packaging, social enterprise recycled and sustainable toilet paper and wooden toothbrushes.

I encourage you to purchase what you need locally or at markets and to look for ethical suppliers, which, in my context, tend to be local and online, utilising carbon-neutral delivery services. Look for ethical and environmental standard accreditations as a guide to businesses that are kind to people and our planet. At church events, move away from disposable plastic and take care to make more considered choices. Whether you are just beginning to take action or preparing for more advanced challenges, you are standing against the pressure of our disposable plastic systems and helping with the mindset and practical reductions for the better.

- As you seek to *live more simply* and dampen the influence of consumer desires to buy and want ever more, your *discipline of generous giving* may have a chance to grow. Financially support global mission partners that are addressing climate change. Consider how you can creatively release your resources for communities most affected or to ease the strains on our natural world. Be a generous steward of money entrusted to you as part of your climate response for this generation and the next.

Creating space for lifestyle change takes preparation and a first step. Return to the insight of where God is calling you. Start with one change that aligns with that calling, and go from there. It may feel counter-cultural or challenging, but please begin with one first step you can take this week. Take the time to map out your practical steps and what your journey could look like from here. You can find a tool to help you plan in the appendix at the end of this book.

Turn your passion for change in our world into an action plan

We have considered how taking actions across the spectrum of our lives and influence matters. We began this journey by exploring our shaping of how God has connected our passions and opportunities and what God may be placing on our hearts.

What's your vision for significant change in our world? What big problems are specifically on your heart? How might you play a constructive part, using your God-given skills and resources?

The following questions may help you reflect and map the problem and the steps you might take to play a constructive part. Allow yourself time to consider how you might contribute your passions, skills and resources. These questions are set out as an additional planning tool in the appendix.[8]

- Where are you feeling prompted to respond to needs in our world? Perhaps there is a particular issue that you are drawn to.
- What significant change do you want to see in response to this need or challenge?
- Can you identify what specific problems need to be addressed to move towards this hopeful change?
- Identify the key individuals or groups that can deliver this change. Consider why they haven't already. Identify who or what influences these gatekeepers.
- Plan five key steps to move in the right direction. Identify who you can collaborate with to organise and problem-solve, and find ways to join existing initiatives for collective impact.
- What signs of progress will you look for after taking your five key steps to show that you are heading in the right direction? When will you check in on this progress?

Congratulations on creating your action plan! As you begin to implement it, remain focused and resilient, and remember to adapt when necessary. Collaboration and innovation are essential, so don't hesitate to connect with others who share your vision. You have the capability to make a difference, and your efforts will have an impact. Stay motivated and continue pushing for the changes our planet needs.

Guiding mentors for the journey

Responding to God's call with our whole lives is a journey made more meaningful by the mentors who exemplify a faithful life. From the writers whose words stir our souls to the everyday saints whose lives serve as sermons of compassion, mentors embody God's call in the language of daily life. In Scripture, we see examples of growing and guiding mentor relationships, such as Barnabas shaping Paul through observational learning and shared ministry (Acts 11; 13), Barnabas and John Mark (Acts 15:37–39), Priscilla and Aquila with Apollos (Acts 18:24–26), and Paul mentoring younger leaders such as Timothy and Titus (2 Corinthians 1:1; 1 Thessalonians 1:1; Titus 1:4). These examples reveal God's good purposes at work through the nurturing, growth and replication among believers that facilitated the spread of the early Church.

We have learned from the models of our contributors, in and through whom we see God's active presence in our world. Our contributors shared their heart yearnings concerning the brokenness of our world, the way their hands have been at work seeking to heal its wounds, and how they see the community of believers at work in God's kingdom. They not only serve as models for action but also embody practices of rest, prayer and renewal. For Katharine Hayhoe, it is drawing near to her heavenly Father in the ministry of nature and community and doing what she loves with the people she loves. Katharine explains that she is fighting for our world because of everything and everyone she loves.[9] Dave Bookless finds spiritual nourishment in the whispers of nature, where daily prayer walks and Bible readings deepen his faith and find expression through his local church. And he draws on the encouragement of growing generations taking up the gospel's call to steward the earth.[10] These are glimpses into holistic lives that model faith in practice.

As we follow the examples set by mentors, we, in turn, shape others, perpetuating a cycle of growth and learning. Mentors remind me of lessons from nature, particularly from the ancient Huon pines found in Tasmania, Australia's southern protected wilderness. These towering, thousand-year-old trees are testaments to resilience and growth, representing some of our planet's oldest plant lineages. I was struck by how a fallen Huon pine branch can give life to a grove of new trees. This reminds me of how mentors plant seeds of wisdom and faith that sprout in the lives of those they encounter. Consider again Paul's words in 1 Corinthians 3:6: 'I planted the seed, Apollos watered it, but God has been making it grow.' In this ecosystem of influence, every faithful action can reach outwards, nurturing change in our world.

Earlier, we imagined what the Church could look like, and turned to individuals who practically model holistic transformation as a guide. It may be that the guidance of a mentor will help you put into action your plan for change and response to the topics explored in this book. Here are some considerations if you are looking for a mentor:

- *Identify a potential mentor:* who in your circle has a vibrant faith, exemplifies godly character and lives with integrity? As we are reminded in 1 Corinthians 11:1, follow a mentor's example as they follow the example of Christ. In light of the failures of some high-profile Christian leaders, identifying a mentor may feel awkward or tinged with cynicism. While perfection is unattainable, seek out individuals who are earnestly pursuing a life you aspire to emulate, and who can positively influence your journey as a follower of Jesus. Consider whether the individuals you admire can nurture your spiritual growth and guide you towards greater obedience to God.
- *Consider church models:* recognise the diverse traditions and expressions of Christian mentorship. Whether through informal guidance and observation, formal mentoring, spiritual direction, coaching or the insights of pastors and elders, each

plays a role in fostering faith, and one might work better for you than others.

- *Set expectations:* reflect on what you hope to gain from mentorship. Consider the time you can commit, the frequency and duration of meetings, your preferred learning style and the areas of your life you wish to develop. Being clear about your expectations will help you communicate your hopes effectively with your prospective mentor.
- *Seek God's guidance:* dedicate time to prayer, asking the Holy Spirit for wisdom, courage and the necessary resources as you search for a role model.

As we are reminded of the importance of mutual encouragement in Hebrews 10:24–25, may we spur one another on towards love and good deeds. May you be blessed in every step you take towards growth under the guidance and love of God.

Reflection

And so we reach our final reflective moment.

Our contemplation inspires us to take steps forward and gain new perspectives.

Visualise yourself standing at the beginning of a path. This path represents your journey towards a safe climate and a healthy environment. The path stretches out before you, but you can see only a short distance ahead.

Reflect on how your choices and actions will influence larger changes and how you can best amplify the impact through collective efforts. Maybe the wisdom you've encountered from across the worldwide Church will guide you, or someone in your life whose faith journey inspires you on your path. Trust in the gifts God has given you as you take steps forward and spread God's justice and compassion.

Recall Psalm 119:105: 'Your word is a lamp for my feet, / a light on my path.'

Picture yourself taking steps on this path.

As you move forward, notice how your vantage point changes.

Perhaps you can support and encourage others in their journey, even when facing challenges. With each step, you can see a little further ahead, like the lamp lighting the path for your feet. Trust that God will reveal more of the path as you continue further on your journey.

Thank God for this time of reflection and guidance.

We lift up our planet in heartfelt prayer.
We come ready to embrace transformative change.
Empower us to create a lasting and positive impact in the face of environmental challenges, caring for our world and ourselves with the love and dedication you have shown us.
We seek your powerful presence to inspire humanity to end harmful habits that damage our earth.
Guide us towards a safer climate future, harnessing the natural power of trees and seas, and doing so swiftly, safely and justly.
Help us adapt to ongoing changes and build resilience for the future, trusting in your infinite wisdom and strength.
May our prayers and actions bring healing and hope to all people and our planet.
Amen.

Conclusion

As we reach the final part of this book, let's revisit the central question that has guided our exploration: What if we wholeheartedly embraced God's call to care for people and our planet? What if we celebrated God's call in our discipleship through every aspect of our lives? This exploration is not just rhetorical; it has been an invitation to deepen our relationship with God, re-examine our purpose and align ourselves with God's vision for the future. We are new creations with renewed hearts and God's Spirit within us. God works to help transform our minds and motivate us towards the good deeds prepared for us.

Imagine the renewal of our world as we truly live out this calling, with the Church as a living organism pulsating with the rhythm of divine purpose and interconnections. We would nurture the seeds of radical followers of Jesus. This vision of the Church is of a vibrant community actively engaging with God's world, not limited to a building or disconnected souls. Let us lean into a future where we contribute to the earth's regeneration, paving the way for renewed health and vitality for the next generation.

As followers of Jesus, we can protect the intricate web of life that God has entrusted to us. Love compels us to drive the urgent changes needed across every level of society, for the sake of all that we hold dear. Facing the greatest challenges of our times requires bold, innovative approaches that diverge from the destructive and extractive ways of the recent past. As we embrace our yearning for God's renewed creation, we cultivate hearts as tender as new leaves for those who suffer, and keep our minds open to the winds of transformation. We move to action that changes lives and enables our natural world to thrive within its God-given limits. While the shape of this action will vary in each of our stories, the goal remains the same: to foster the flourishing of life on earth and the joy that comes with it.

Our generation stands at a crossroads, holding the power to avert climate catastrophe and to make decisive strides for the benefit of all generations. As I take in the untamed beauty of the Australian bush while my children play outside, I reflect on the legacy we will choose for the world of 2050, the year we need to reach net-zero emissions for a safer climate future. What will the impacts and temperatures be like in a world my sons will call home? Our legacy must be one of proactive stewardship and action. Watching my boys quickly grow, I recognise how fast the next decade approaches and that the time for transformation is now. This coming decade is filled with opportunities for meaningful change to reshape our systems and lifestyles. We can choose to act now, allowing our children and theirs to cherish our natural world.

Our journey has revealed countless ways to foster God's kingdom – spreading justice, peace and abundance for all. In contemplation, we've listened to God's voice and discerned a mission entrusted to each of us. The enormity of our hurting, warming world can seem overwhelming, but we can take hold of models of a promising, tangible future, enabling us to shift away from the paralysis of indifference or overwhelm. Through our biblical values, the inspiration of stories and ideas, the guidance of mentors and tools for action, we can each play a meaningful part in what comes next.

Let us move forward with courage. In every act of conservation, pursuit of righteousness and kindness, we collectively embody God's likeness and calling towards God's kingdom on earth. Our hope rests in God and in the work he empowers us to do. So let us embrace this mission with open hearts, ready to act with urgent hopefulness for God's renewed creation, free of poverty.

Together we close in prayer:

Heavenly Father,
As we conclude this book, we embrace your call to care for people and our planet.
Deepen our relationship with you and guide us in fulfilling your vision for the future.
Transform us as we eagerly pursue the good works you have set before us.
We welcome a vibrant vision for your Church, actively engaging with the world.
Grant our generation the courage to stand up for the necessary transformations to meet the climate challenge.
Holy Spirit, would your love drive us to seek climate justice and pursue innovative approaches, leaving a legacy of renewal.

Now to him who is able to do immeasurably more than all we ask or imagine, according to his power that is at work within us, to him be glory in the church and in Christ Jesus throughout all generations, for ever and ever! Amen.[1]

Appendix
Make plans and respond to God's call

Planning for purposeful living

Where am I noticing God's calling to make changes in my day-to-day life?

This week:

- What specific actions can I take this week to align with this calling?

Next steps:

- What are the next steps I can take to respond to this calling?

Steps by one month:

- What milestones do I want to achieve within the next month?

Support and accountability moving forward:

- Who can I rely on for support and accountability as I make these changes?

Sharing my journey:

- Who in my network can I share my motivations and actions with regarding climate change?

Planning for change in our world

Where am I feeling prompted to respond to needs in our world?

Vision for change:

- What is the significant change I want to see in response to this need or challenge?

Identifying problems:

- What specific problems need to be addressed to move towards this hopeful change?

Gatekeepers:

- Who are the key individuals or groups that can deliver this change?
- What influences these gatekeepers?

Action steps:

- What are five key steps I can take to move in the right direction?
- Can I collaborate with others to organise and problem-solve towards the desired change?

Signs of progress:

- After taking these five steps, what indicators will show that I am heading in the right direction?

Continue your journey
Resources for further exploration

Anderson, H., *Turning of Days: Lessons from nature, season and spirit* (Chicago: Moody, 2021).

- *The author transports us to the Blue Ridge Mountains in Virginia, guiding us in a new way of seeing God at work in our natural world, season by season.*

Berry, R. J., and L. S. Meitzner Yoder (eds), *John Stott on Creation Care* (London: IVP, 2021).

- *This impressive collection is for those ready to go deeper and brings together John Stott's writings on creation care and his passion for connecting the environment with Christian discipleship.*

Bookless, D., *God Doesn't Do Waste: Redeeming the whole of life* (Nottingham: IVP, 2010).

- *Dave's journey of conviction and action is told as an engaging story.*

Bookless, D., *Planetwise: Dare to care for God's world* (Nottingham: IVP, 2008).

- *Dave's popular theology book has been translated into multiple languages and builds accessible biblical knowledge of creation care.*

Bookless, D., and Renew Our World, *Making a World of Difference* (2023): www.renewourworld.net/resources

- *This short book, available for free, is a resource for church leaders and members. It provides a biblical understanding of climate and nature crises with discussion questions and stories of Church action.*

Farron, T., *A Mucky Business: Why Christians should get involved in politics* (London: IVP, 2022).

- *Politicians of faith unpack how they are Christians in the political world, seeking to equip others to engage with politics effectively.*

Gower, R., and R. Walker, *The Hopeful Activist: Discovering the vital change you were made to bring* (London: SPCK, 2024).

- *Written by practitioners, this positive guide builds knowledge and translates it into action, starting with how to begin, where to go and how to sustain the journey.*

Hayhoe, K., *Saving Us: A climate scientist's case for hope and healing in a divided world* (New York: Simon & Schuster, 2021).

- *Katharine's bestseller provides tools for conversations that build common ground and impact our networks as we act with hope on climate change.*

Hayhoe, K., and Tearfund Scotland, *Christianity and climate change* (film series) (Tearfund, 2020): www.tearfund.org/campaigns/christianity-and-climate-change-film-series

- *This highly recommended video and discussion series is ideal for small groups and churches just starting to grapple with climate change.*

Lausanne Movement Global Classroom, *Creation Care* (film series): www.lausanne.org/global-classroom/creation-care-episode

- *This excellent video series features leading Christian thinkers and practitioners, including Ruth, Dave and Katharine, and builds biblical knowledge and the case for holistic discipleship, with an accompanying guide for further exploration.*

Meitzner Yoder, L. S. (ed.), *Living Radical Discipleship: Inspired by John Stott* (Carlisle: Langham Global Library, 2021).

- *This excellent collection helps us integrate our discipleship into every sphere of life and includes a chapter by Kuki and a foreword by Ruth.*

Rinaudo, T., *The Forest Underground: Hope for a planet in crisis* (Melbourne: ISCAST, 2022).

- *Full of pictures and stories, this beautiful book traces Tony's life journey and the growth of the forest underground movement.*

Tearfund, 'Restorative Revolution: Bible Studies': https://learn.tearfund.org/en/resources/series/restorative-revolution/restorative-revolution-bible-studies

- *This Bible study resource is written by young theologians from different continents to help churches engage with the Restorative Revolution vision for a restorative economy meeting twenty-first-century challenges.*

Valerio, R., *L Is for Lifestyle: Christian living that doesn't cost the earth* (rev. edn; London: IVP, 2019).

- *Ruth's popular book is a key resource to apply responsible faith choices through an A–Z of sustainable and just living.*

Taking action

Action supplement from *Awhi Mai Awhi Atu: Women in Creation Care*: https://www.conversations.net.nz/awhi-women-in-creation-care.html

- *For eighty-one transferable action ideas across different domains of life; free to download.*

Christian Climate Action: https://christianclimateaction.org

- *For direct non-violent prayer and action as a Christian response.*

Climate Vigil Songs, album by The Porter's Gate (2022) (available on Spotify or via https://www.portersgateworship.com)

- *For worship resources that help shift the songs we sing.*

Dave Bookless, Lausanne and World Evangelical Alliance, *The Pollinator*, Creation Care Network News: https://wea-sc.org/en/the-pollinator

- *To stay informed about Christian creation care opportunities and actions.*

Green Anglicans: www.greenanglicans.org

- *For resources and actions led by young people in Southern Africa.*

Katharine Hayhoe's website: www.katharinehayhoe.com

- *To go deeper into resources and constructive conversations led by Katharine.*

Micah Australia: www.micahaustralia.org

- *For political advocacy on issues of justice and poverty with the coalition of Christian international development organisations.*

Renew Our World: www.renewourworld.net

- *To join an exciting Christian movement of Christians taking action and praying for a fairer world with expressions in more than twenty countries, alongside Kuki, Dave and others who have contributed to this book.*

Ruth Valerio's website: www.ruthvalerio.net

- *To stay up to date with Ruth's thought leadership and practical applications.*

Season of Creation: https://seasonofcreation.org/

- *For resourcing your local church each September to participate in the worldwide Season of Creation.*

Bibliography

Books

Anderson, H., *Turning of Days: Lessons from nature, season and spirit* (Chicago: Moody, 2021).

Attenborough, D., *A Life on Our Planet: My witness statement and a vision for the future* (London: Penguin Random House, 2020).

Berry, R. J., and L. S. Meitzner Yoder (eds), *John Stott on Creation Care* (London: IVP, 2021).

Bird, M., *Romans*, The Story of God Bible Commentary (Grand Rapids: Zondervan, 2016).

Bookless, D., *God Doesn't Do Waste: Redeeming the whole of life* (Nottingham: IVP, 2010).

——, *Planetwise: Dare to care for God's world* (Nottingham: IVP, 2008).

Brueggemann, W., *Genesis*, Interpretation: A Bible Commentary for Teaching and Preaching (Louisville: John Knox Press, 2010).

Cornford, J., *Coming Back to Earth: Essays on the Church, climate change, cities, agriculture and eating* (Sydney: Morning Star, 2016).

——, *Coming Home: Discipleship, ecology and everyday economics* (Sydney: Morning Star, 2019).

Costello, T., *A Lot with a Little* (Melbourne: Hardie Grant Books, 2019).

Delgado, S., *Love in a Time of Climate Change: Honoring creation, establishing justice* (Minneapolis: Fortress, 2017).

de Mello, A., *Sadhana: A Way to God; Christian exercises in Eastern form* (Melbourne: Harper Collins, 1998).

Farron, T., *A Mucky Business: Why Christians should get involved in politics* (London: IVP, 2022).

Figueres, C., and T. Rivett-Carnac, *The Future We Choose: Surviving the climate crisis* (London: Manilla Press, 2020).

Ganz, M., *Why David Sometimes Wins: Leadership, organization, and strategy in the California farm worker movement* (Oxford: Oxford University Press, 2009).

Gower, R., and R. Walker, *The Hopeful Activist: Discovering the vital change you were made to bring* (London: SPCK, 2024).

Hartl, J., *Simply Pray* (Edinburgh: Muddy Pearl, 2018).

Hayhoe, K., *Saving Us: A climate scientist's case for hope and healing in a divided world* (New York: Simon & Schuster, 2021).

Holtam, N., *Sleepers Wake: Getting serious about climate change; The Archbishop of York's Advent book 2022* (London: SPCK, 2022).

Huntley, R., *How to Talk about Climate Change in a Way That Makes a Difference* (Sydney: Murdoch Books, 2020).

Keller, T., *Generous Justice: How God's grace makes us just* (London: Hodder & Stoughton, 2010).

Malcolm, H. (ed.), *Words for a Dying World: Stories of grief and courage from the global church* (London: SCM, 2020).

Meitzner Yoder, L. S. (ed.), *Living Radical Discipleship: Inspired by John Stott* (Carlisle: Langham Global Library, 2021).

Moo, D. J., *The Letters to the Colossians and to Philemon*, The Pillar New Testament Commentary (Grand Rapids: Eerdmans, 2008).

Moo, D. J., and J. A. Moo, *Creation Care: A biblical theology of the natural world*, Biblical Theology for Life series (Grand Rapids: Zondervan, 2018).

Newbigin, L., *Foolishness to the Greeks: Gospel and Western culture* (London: SPCK, 1986).

Pope, M., and C. Dawson, *A Climate of Hope: Church and mission in a warming world* (Melbourne: UNOH, 2014).

Purdie, S. (ed.), *Awhi Mai Awhi Atu: Women in creation care* (Wellington: Philip Garside Books, 2022).

Raworth, K., *Doughnut Economics: Seven ways to think like a 21st-century economist* (London: Random House, 2019).

Richter, S. L., *Stewards of Eden: What Scripture says about the environment and why it matters* (Downers Grove: IVP Academic, 2020).

Rinaudo, T., *The Forest Underground: Hope for a planet in crisis* (Melbourne: ISCAST, 2022).

Rose, A., *Madlands: A journey to change the mind of a climate sceptic* (Melbourne: Melbourne University Press, 2012).

Sayers, M., *Disappearing Church: From cultural relevance to gospel resilience* (Chicago: Moody, 2016).

Seaton, C., *Whose Earth?* (Cambridge: Crossway, 1992).

Stone, S., *Tarry Awhile: Wisdom from Black spirituality for people of faith; The Archbishop of Canterbury's Lent book 2024* (London: SPCK, 2023).

Stott, J., *The Birds Our Teachers: Essays in orni-theology* (London: Three's Company, 1999).

——, *The Radical Disciple: Wholehearted Christian living* (London: IVP, 2010).

Thunberg, G., *The Climate Book* (London: Penguin Random House, 2022).

Valerio, R., *L Is for Lifestyle: Christian living that doesn't cost the earth* (rev. edn; London: IVP, 2019).

——, *Saying Yes to Life: The Archbishop of Canterbury's Lent book 2020* (London: SPCK, 2019).

Warren, T. H., *Liturgy of the Ordinary: Sacred practices in everyday life* (Downers Grove: IVP, 2016).

——, *Prayer in the Night: For those who work or watch or weep* (Downers Grove: IVP, 2021).

Watkin, C., *Thinking through Creation: Genesis 1 and 2 as tools of cultural critique* (Phillipsburg: P&R, 2017).

Williams, R., *Being Disciples: Essentials of the Christian life* (London: SPCK, 2016).

Wright, C., *'Here Are Your Gods': Faithful discipleship in idolatrous times* (London: IVP, 2020).

Wright, N. T., *Surprised by Hope: Rethinking heaven, the resurrection, and the mission of the Church* (London: SPCK, 2008).

Wytsma, K., *Pursuing Justice: The call to live and die for bigger things* (Nashville: Thomas Nelson, 2013).

Zaki A., and N. Presa (eds), *Now to God Who Is Able: Vocation, justice, and ministry; Essays in honor of Mark Labberton* (Eugene: Wipf & Stock, 2023).

Interviews

Bhagwan, J. (interviewee). Video call. Interview conducted by J. Knight, 30 August 2023.

Bookless, D. (interviewee). In person and recorded. Interview conducted by J. Knight, 16 March 2023.

Felistar (interviewee, surname withheld). In person and recorded. Interview conducted by J. Knight with an interpreter, 10 March 2023.

Hayhoe, K. (interviewee). Video call. Interview conducted by J. Knight, 8 September 2023.

Minniecon, R. (interviewee). Video call. Interview conducted by J. Knight, 16 August 2023.

Rinaudo, T. (interviewee). In person and by email. Interview conducted by J. Knight, 27 January 2024 and 10 February 2024.

Rokhum, K. (interviewee). Video call. Interview conducted by J. Knight, 24 January 2024.

Samuel, C. B. (interviewee). Video call. Interview conducted by J. Knight, 8 September 2023.

Valerio, R. (interviewee). Video call. Interview conducted by J. Knight, 24 August 2022.

Wright, N. T. Video call. Facilitated discussion with *Soul Tread* supporters, including J. Knight, conducted by R. Lopez, 15 July 2021.

Journals, papers and reports

Bookless, D., and Renew Our World, *Making a World of Difference* (2023): www.renewourworld.net/resources (accessed 1 January 2024).

DeBorst, R. P., '"Unlikely Partnerships": Global discipleship in the twenty-first century', *Transformation* 28.4 (2011), pp. 241–52: https://doi.org/10.1177/0265378811417531 (accessed 13 June 2024).

Fileta, J. (ed.), *Live Justly: Global edition* (Portland: Micah Challenge and Tearfund, 2017).

Kirkpatrick, D., 'C. René Padilla and the Origins of Integral Mission in Post-War Latin America', *The Journal of Ecclesiastical History* 67.2 (April 2016), pp. 351–71.

Knight, J., 'Creation Justice: Our calling to care for people and God's planet', *Soul Tread* 4 (Spring 2021), pp. 66–71.

Lee, H., and J. Romero (eds), 'Summary for Policymakers', in IPCC, *Climate Change 2023: Synthesis report; contribution of Working Groups I, II and III to the Sixth Assessment Report of the Intergovernmental Panel on Climate Change* (Geneva: IPCC, 2023), pp. 1–34: https://www.ipcc.ch/report/sixth-assessment-report-cycle/ (accessed 20 December 2024).

Moo, D. J., 'Nature in the New Creation: New Testament eschatology and the environment', *Journal of the Evangelical Theological Society* 49.3 (Sep. 2006), pp. 449–88.

Padilla, C. R., 'Holistic Mission', Occasional Paper, Lausanne Movement: https://lausanne.org/occasional-paper/holistic-mission (accessed 5 January 2025).

Palassio, C., 'Convincing People That Change Is Possible by "Painting the Beautiful Tomorrow"', The Philanthropist Journal, 31 July 2023: https://thephilanthropist.ca/2023/07/convincing-people-that-change-is-possible-by-painting-the-beautiful-tomorrow (accessed 27 November 2024).

Spencer, L., *How to Talk about Economics* (Australian Progress, version 1.0 (n.d.)), pp. 3–4: https://www.australianprogress.org.au/resources/how-to-talk-about-economics (accessed 19 August 2024).

Tearfund, 'Advocacy Toolkit – a Roots guide': https://learn.tearfund.org/en/resources/series/roots-guides/advocacy-toolkit--a-roots-guide (accessed 30 July 2024).

——, 'The Restorative Economy: Completing our unfinished millennium jubilee' (2015): https://www.tearfund.ie/wp-content/uploads/2018/09/Restorative-Economy-Summary-Report-Tearfund.pdf (accessed 21 March 2024).

——, 'Restorative Revolution: Bible Studies': https://learn.tearfund.org/en/resources/series/restorative-revolution/restorative-revolution-bible-studies.

——, 'Restorative Revolution: Report': https://learn.tearfund.org/en/resources/series/restorative-revolution/restorative-revolution-report.

Tearfund and Youthscape Centre for Research, 'Burning Down the House: How the Church could lose young people over climate inaction', p. 2: https://wearetearfund.org/burning-down-the-house/ (accessed 21 March 2023).

Tearfund Australia, 'For All Creation', campaign paper: www.tearfund.org.au/forallcreation/paper.

——, *They Shall Inherit the Earth: 2022 Tearfund Climate Report* (Blackburn Victoria: Tearfund Australia, 2022): tearfund.link/crf (accessed 21 March 2023).

UnitingWorld, 'A Theology of Disaster Resilience in a Changing Climate', Framework Paper with Australian Aid and CANDO, 2019.

Whitmore-Williams, S. C., C. M. Manning, K. Krygsman and M. Speiser, *Mental Health and Our Changing Climate: Impacts, implications, and guidance* (Washington, D.C.: American Psychological Association, and ecoAmerica, 2017): https://www.apa.org/news/press/releases/2017/03/mental-health-climate.pdf (accessed 21 March 2024).

World Council of Churches, 'Otin Tai Declaration', 6–11 March 2004: https://www.oikoumene.org/resources/documents/otin-tai-declaration.

Websites and articles

24-7 Prayer, Tearfund and Renew Our World, 'How to Pray for Climate Change' and 'Pray for the Climate': https://www.renewourworld.net/resources (accessed 21 March 2024).

Anglican Overseas Aid: www.anglicanoverseasaid.org.au (accessed 26 August 2025).

The Archbishop of Canterbury, 'Archbishop Presents Pastor Ray Minniecon with Lambeth Award', 11 October 2022: www.archbishopofcanterbury.org/priorities/archbishops-commission-families-and-households/news/archbishop-presents-pastor-ray (accessed 21 March 2024).

A Rocha UK, 'Climate Anxiety and the Church': https://arocha.org.uk/climate-anxiety-and-the-Church/ (accessed 21 March 2024).

ASO Communications, 'Mobilizing towards Climate Justice': https://asocommunications.com/messaging_guides/mobilizing-towards-climate-justice/ (accessed 26 August 2025).

Australian Geographic, 'DNA Confirms Aboriginal Culture One of Earth's Oldest', 23 September 2011: www.australiangeographic.com.au/news/2011/09/dna-confirms-aboriginal-culture-one-of-earths-oldest/ (accessed 5 June 2024).

Australian Psychological Association, 'Coping with Climate Change Distress': https://psychology.org.au/for-the-public/psychology-topics/climate-change-psychology/coping-with-climate-change-distress (accessed 30 July 2024).

Australians Together, 'The Stolen Generations: The forcible removal of First Nations children from their families': https://australianstogether.org.au/discover-and-learn/our-history/stolen-generations (accessed 21 March 2024).

Bhagwan, J., 'Two Decades after Landmark Declaration – Pacific churches take a stronger stand for climate justice', Toda Peace Institute, 18 July 2024: https://toda.org/global-outlook/2024/

two-decades-after-landmark-declaration-pacific-churches-take-a-stronger-stand-for-climate-justice.html (accessed 13 December 2024).

Bible Project, 'Heaven & Earth': https://bibleproject.com/explore/video/heaven-and-earth/?utm_source=web_social_share&medium=shared_video (accessed 21 March 2024).

—— 'Justice': https://bibleproject.com/explore/video/justice/ (accessed 21 March 2024).

Bookless, D., J. Kwong, S. Appiah-Kubi and J. Solano, 'Creation Care', Lausanne Movement: www.lausanne.org/report/sustainable/creation-care (accessed 6 June 2024).

Bringing Them Home, 'Historical Context – Ancient History', Australian Human Rights Commission: https://bth.humanrights.gov.au/significance/historical-context-ancient-history (accessed 5 June 2024).

Christian Aid: https://www.christianaid.org.uk/ (accessed 26 August 2025).

Christian Climate Action: https://christianclimateaction.org/resources/climate-grief-and-anxiety/ (accessed 21 March 2024).

The Communion Forest: https://www.communionforest.org/ (accessed 26 August 2025).

Daughtry, S., 'Season of Creation – prayers and resources', ABM 2023: https://www.abmission.org/resources/fifth-mark-of-mission/ (accessed 1 April 2024).

Eco Church scheme, part of A Rocha UK: https://ecochurch.arocha.org.uk/ (accessed 1 August 2024).

Endara, E., 'Every Action Matters: A Q&A with climate scientist, Katharine Hayhoe', 23 November 2021, Oxfam America: https://www.oxfamamerica.org/explore/stories/every-action-matters-a-qa-with-climate-scientist-katharine-hayhoe/ (accessed 21 March 2024).

Grace Capital City church, Washington D.C.: https://www.gracecapitalcity.com (accessed 27 December 2024).

Green Anglicans: https://www.greenanglicans.org/ (accessed 26 August 2025).

Greig, P., 'Sabbath Blessing': www.dirtyglory.org/new-page-3 (accessed 21 March 2023).

IPCC (The Intergovernmental Panel on Climate Change): https://www.ipcc.ch/ (accessed 26 August 2025).

Lausanne Movement, 'The Cape Town Commitment': https://lausanne.org/content/ctc/ctcommitment#p1–7 (accessed 21 March 2024).

——, 'Integral Mission': www.lausanne.org/network/integral-mission (accessed 6 June 2024).

Langham Publishing, 'CB Samuel', https://langhamliterature.org/author-bio?author_id=10906 (accessed 6 June 2024).

Micah Global, 'Micah Network Declaration on Integral Mission': https://d1c2gz5q23tkk0.cloudfront.net/shrine_store/uploads/networks/1730/page_customizables/385755/5b3630efcfd41a0e1df7745cc2ba8735.pdf_1662641257 (accessed 6 June 2024)

NAIITS (formerly the North American Institute for Indigenous Theological Studies): www.naiits.com/about/ (accessed 6 June 2024).

Oxfam, 'Survival of the Richest': www.oxfam.org/en/research/survival-richest (accessed 16 January 2023).

Pattee, E., 'Leading Climate Scientist Katharine Hayhoe: "You have the ability to use your voice"', *The Guardian*, 10 November 2021: https://www.theguardian.com/environment/2021/nov/10/katharine-hayoe-climate-change-interview (accessed 21 March 2024).

Paulson, M., 'Inequality as a Religious Issue: A conversation with the Archbishop of Canterbury': The *New York Times*, 23 January 2015, https://www.nytimes.com/2015/01/24/us/archbishop-of-canterbury-inequality.html (accessed 21 March 2024).

Pew Research Center, 'Global Christianity: A report on the size and distribution of the world's Christian population': https://www.pewresearch.org/religion/2011/12/19/global-christianity-exec (accessed 22 August 2024).

Preaching for God's World: https://preachingforgodsworld.org/ (accessed 26 August 2025).

Project Drawdown: https://drawdown.org/ (accessed 26 August 2025).

Raworth, K., 'Exploring Doughnut Economics': www.kateraworth.com/doughnut/ (accessed 21 March 2024).

Renew Our World: https://www.renewourworld.net/ (accessed 13 December 2024).

Save the Children, 'Survey Reveals Scale of Climate Anxiety among British Children on Eve of Cop27', 4 November 2022: https://www.savethechildren.org.uk/news/media-centre/press-releases/survey-reveals-scale-of-climate-anxiety-among-british-children (accessed 30 July 2024).

Schlöndorff, V. (director), *The Forest Maker* (also known as Ormanların Kurtarıcısı), documentary (zero one film with Volksfilm, 2021): https://www.zeroone.de/en/movies/forestmaker/ (accessed 8 August 2024).

Season of Creation: https://seasonofcreation.org/ (accessed 26 August 2025).

Solano, J., 'The Commodification of the Sacred: A Reflection from COP28', AllCreation,org: www.allcreation.org/home/commodification (accessed 6 June 2024).

Stockholm Resilience Centre, Stockholm University, 'Planetary Boundaries': https://www.stockholmresilience.org/research/planetary-boundaries.html (accessed 21 March 2024).

UN Environment Programme, '10 Ways You Can Help Fight the Climate Crisis': https://www.unep.org/news-and-stories/story/10-ways-you-can-help-fight-climate-crisis (accessed 21 March 2024).

United Nations, 'Climate Change': https://www.un.org/en/global-issues/climate-change (accessed 2 January 2025).

UN News, 'Hottest July Ever Signals "Era of Global Boiling Has Arrived" Says UN Chief', 27 July 2023: https://news.un.org/en/story/2023/07/1139162 (accessed 21 June 2024).

UN Sustainable Development Goals, 'Be the Change': https://www.un.org/sustainabledevelopment/be-the-change (accessed 22 August 2024).

Wilson, S., 'Rewilding Scotland', *The Scotsman*, 11 January 2021 (no longer available online).

World Evangelical Alliance, 'Defining the Character of the Kingdom of God by Rev. CB Samuel (Devotional 1)', YouTube, 8 November 2019: https://youtu.be/rqMBadPoVw4 (accessed 21 March 2024).

World Meteorological Organization, 'Africa Suffers Disproportionately from Climate Change', 4 September 2023: www.wmo.int/news/media-centre/africa-suffers-disproportionately-from-climate-change (accessed 4 September 2023).

——, 'Global Temperature Is Likely to Exceed 1.5°C above Pre-industrial Level Temporarily in Next 5 Years', 5 June 2024: https://wmo.int/news/media-centre/global-temperature-likely-exceed-15degc-above-pre-industrial-level-temporarily-next-5-years (accessed 27 December 2024).

Notes

Introduction

1 J. Stott, *The Radical Disciple: Wholehearted Christian living* (London: IVP, 2010).

2 R. Williams, *Being Disciples: Essentials of the Christian life* (London: SPCK, 2016), p. 1.

1. Call: God's plan for all creation

1 R. Valerio (interviewee), video call; interview conducted by J. Knight, 24 August 2022.

2 W. Brueggemann, *Genesis*, Interpretation: A Bible Commentary for Teaching and Preaching (Louisville: John Knox Press, 2010), p. 25.

3 R. J. Berry and L. S. Meitzner Yoder (eds), *John Stott on Creation Care* (London: IVP, 2021), p. 56.

4 J. Stott, *The Birds Our Teachers: Essays in orni-theology* (London: Three's Company, 1999).

5 Stott, *The Birds Our Teachers*, p. 10.

6 M. Luther, 'The Sermon on the Mount', in *Luther's Works*, vol. 21, tr. J. Pelikan (Saint Louis, MO: Concordia, 1956 (1521)), pp. 197–8, quoted in Stott, *The Birds Our Teachers*, p. 10.

7 Valerio (interview).

8 K. Hayhoe (interviewee), video call; interview conducted by J. Knight, 8 September 2023.

9 D. Bookless, *Planetwise: Dare to care for God's world* (Nottingham: IVP, 2008), pp. 30–33.

10 See D. J. Moo and J. A. Moo, *Creation Care: A biblical theology of the natural world*, Biblical Theology for Life series (Grand Rapids: Zondervan, 2018), p. 69.

11 Valerio (interview).
12 S. L. Richter, *Stewards of Eden: What Scripture says about the environment and why it matters* (Downers Grove: IVP Academic, 2020), p. 95.
13 See Moo and Moo, *Creation Care*, p. 103.
14 R. P. DeBorst, 'Just Worship: Responding to the cry of the people and the earth', in A. Zaki and N. Presa (eds), *Now to God Who Is Able: Vocation, justice, and ministry; Essays in honor of Mark Labberton* (Eugene: Wifp & Stock, 2023), p. 56.
15 Valerio (interview).
16 See M. Bird, *Romans*, The Story of God Bible Commentary (Grand Rapids: Zondervan, 2016), p. 277.
17 See Moo and Moo, *Creation Care*, p. 142.
18 See D. J. Moo, *The Letters to the Colossians and to Philemon*, The Pillar New Testament Commentary (Grand Rapids: Eerdmans, 2008), p. 137.
19 D. Bookless (interviewee), in person and voice recording; interview conducted by J. Knight, 16 March 2023.
20 Bookless (interview).
21 Bookless (interview).
22 N. T. Wright, video call; facilitated discussion with *Soul Tread* supporters conducted by R. Lopez, 15 July 2021; and J. Knight, 'Creation Justice: Our calling to care for people and God's planet', *Soul Tread* 4 (Spring 2021), pp. 69–70.
23 Wright (video call); and Knight, 'Creation Justice', pp. 69–70.
24 Wright (video call); and Knight, 'Creation Justice', pp. 69–70.
25 Berry and Yoder, *John Stott*, p. 88.
26 Lausanne Movement, 'The Cape Town Commitment': https://lausanne.org/content/ctc/ctcommitment#p1-7 (accessed 21 March 2024). For more on creation care, see Lausanne Movement: https://lausanne.org/.
27 DeBorst, 'Just Worship', p. 56.
28 T. Keller, *Generous Justice: How God's grace makes us just* (London: Hodder & Stoughton, 2010), p. 93.
29 World Evangelical Alliance, 'Defining the Character of the Kingdom of God by Rev. CB Samuel (Devotional 1)', YouTube, 8 November 2019: https://youtu.be/rqMBadPoVw4 (accessed 21 March 2024).

30 J. Bhagwan (interviewee), video call; interview conducted by J. Knight, 30 August 2023.

31 DeBorst, 'Just Worship', p. 62.

32 R. P. DeBorst, '"Unlikely Partnerships": Global discipleship in the twenty-first century', *Transformation* 28.4 (2011), pp. 241–52: https://doi.org/10.1177/0265378811417531 (accessed 13 June 2024).

2. Response: holistic transformation

1 Micah Global, 'Micah Network Declaration on Integral Mission': https://d1c2gz5q23tkk0.cloudfront.net/shrine_store/uploads/networks/1730/page_customizables/385755/5b3630efcfd41a0e1df7745cc2ba8735.pdf_1662641257 (accessed 6 June 2024).

2 S. Wilson, 'Rewilding Scotland', *The Scotsman*, 11 January 2021 (no longer available online).

3 M. Sayers, *Disappearing Church: From cultural relevance to gospel resilience* (Chicago: Moody, 2016).

4 C. B. Samuel (interviewee), video call; interview conducted by J. Knight, 8 September 2023.

5 See Micah Global, 'Micah Network Declaration'; Lausanne Movement, 'Integral Mission': https://lausanne.org/network/integral-mission (accessed 6 June 2024); and Langham Publishing, 'CB Samuel', https://langhamliterature.org/author-bio?author_id=10906 (accessed 6 June 2024).

6 D. Kirkpatrick, 'C. René Padilla and the Origins of Integral Mission in Post-War Latin America', *The Journal of Ecclesiastical History* 67.2 (April 2016), pp. 351–71.

7 John Stott also provided foundational leadership and engaged in vital conversations in the 1960s and 1970s that continued in various forms in the following decades. For further discussion, see L. S. Meitzner Yoder (ed.), *Living Radical Discipleship: Inspired by John Stott* (Carlisle: Langham Global Library, 2021).

8 Samuel (interview).

9 Bhagwan (interview).

10 Bhagwan (interview).

11 J. Bhagwan, 'Two Decades after Landmark Declaration – Pacific

churches take a stronger stand for climate justice', Toda Peace Institute, 18 July 2024: https://toda.org/global-outlook/2024/two-decades-after-landmark-declaration-pacific-churches-take-a-stronger-stand-for-climate-justice.html (accessed 13 December 2024).

12 Bhagwan (interview); see also the climate and disaster preparation work of Anglican Overseas Aid in the Pacific, 'Exemplifying the CAN DO Spirit in Soloman *[sic]* Islands': https://anglicanoverseasaid.org.au/2024/11/05/exemplifying-the-can-do-spirit-in-soloman-islands/ (accessed 13 December 2024).

13 Hayhoe (interview).

14 Pew Research Center, 'Global Christianity: A report on the size and distribution of the world's Christian population': https://www.pewresearch.org/religion/2011/12/19/global-christianity-exec/ (accessed 22 August 2024).

15 Renew Our World: https://www.renewourworld.net/ (accessed 13 December 2024).

16 See K. Rokhum, 'Loving Our Neighbour in God's World', in Meitzner Yoder, *Living Radical Discipleship*, pp. 79–92.

17 K. Rokhum (interviewee), video call; interview conducted by J. Knight, 24 January 2024.

18 C. R. Padilla, 'Holistic Mission', Occasional Paper, Lausanne Movement: https://lausanne.org/occasional-paper/holistic-mission (accessed 5 January 2025).

19 See Eco Church scheme, part of A Rocha UK: https://ecochurch.arocha.org.uk/ (accessed 1 August 2024).

20 Valerio (interview).

21 See Season of Creation: https://seasonofcreation.org/ (accessed 26 August 2025).

22 See Green Anglicans: https://www.greenanglicans.org/; and Preaching for God's World: https://preachingforgodsworld.org/ (accessed 26 August 2025).

23 The Communion Forest: https://www.communionforest.org/ (accessed 26 August 2025).

24 T. Rinaudo (interviewee), in person and by email; interview conducted by J. Knight, 27 January 2024 and 10 February 2024.

25 Rinaudo (interview).

3. Call: describing and naming the problem

1 UN News, 'Hottest July Ever Signals "Era of Global Boiling Has Arrived" Says UN Chief', 27 July 2023: https://news.un.org/en/story/2023/07/1139162 (accessed 21 June 2024).

2 World Meteorological Organization, 'Global Temperature Is Likely to Exceed 1.5°C above Pre-industrial Level Temporarily in Next 5 Years', 5 June 2024: https://wmo.int/media/news/global-temperature-likely-exceed-15degc-above-pre-industrial-level-temporarily-next-5-years (accessed 27 December 2024).

3 See United Nations, 'Climate Change': https://www.un.org/en/global-issues/climate-change (accessed 2 January 2025).

4 H. Lee and J. Romero (eds), 'Summary for Policymakers', in IPCC, *Climate Change 2023: Synthesis report; Contribution of Working Groups I, II and III to the Sixth Assessment Report of the Intergovernmental Panel on Climate Change* (Geneva: IPCC, 2023), p. 25: https://www.ipcc.ch/report/sixth-assessment-report-cycle/ (accessed 20 December 2024).

5 Lee and Romero, 'Summary for Policymakers', p. 7.

6 See K. Raworth, *Doughnut Economics: Seven ways to think like a 21st-century economist* (London: Random House, 2019); and K. Raworth, 'Exploring Doughnut Economics': www.kateraworth.com/doughnut/ (accessed 21 March 2024).

7 Oxfam, 'Survival of the Richest': https://www.oxfam.org/en/research/survival-richest (accessed 16 January 2023).

8 G. Thunberg, *The Climate Book* (London: Penguin Random House, 2022), p. 3.

9 See Raworth, *Doughnut Economics*; and Raworth, 'Exploring Doughnut Economics'.

10 Tearfund, 'The Restorative Economy: Completing our unfinished millennium jubilee' (2015): https://learn.tearfund.org/en/resources/policy-reports/the-restorative-economy (accessed 21 March 2024).

11 Stockholm Resilience Centre, Stockholm University, 'Planetary Boundaries': https://www.stockholmresilience.org/research/planetary-boundaries.html (accessed 21 March 2024).

12 Stockholm Resilience Centre, 'Planetary Boundaries'.
13 D. Attenborough, *A Life on Our Planet: My witness statement and a vision for the future* (London: Penguin Random House, 2020), p. 6.
14 C. Figueres and T. Rivett-Carnac, *The Future We Choose: Surviving the climate crisis* (London: Manilla Press, 2020), p. 50.
15 See Richter, *Stewards of Eden*; and S. Stone, *Tarry Awhile: Wisdom from Black spirituality for people of faith; The Archbishop of Canterbury's Lent book 2024* (London: SPCK, 2023).
16 N. T. Wright, *God in Public*, p. 111, quoted in T. Farron, *A Mucky Business: Why Christians should get involved in politics* (London: IVP, 2022), p. 85.
17 See C. Wright, *'Here Are Your Gods': Faithful discipleship in idolatrous times* (London: IVP, 2020).
18 R. Minniecon (interviewee), video call; interview conducted by J. Knight, 16 August 2023.
19 Minniecon (interview).
20 Hayhoe (interview).
21 Hayhoe (interview).
22 Hayhoe (interview).
23 Bookless (interview).
24 Bhagwan (interview).
25 L. Spencer, *How to Talk about Economics* (Australian Progress, version 1.0 (n.d.)), pp. 3–4: https://www.australianprogress.org.au/resources/how-to-talk-about-economics (accessed 19 August 2024).
26 Tearfund and Youthscape Centre for Research, 'Burning Down the House: How the Church could lose young people over climate inaction', p. 2: https://wearetearfund.org/burning-down-the-house/ (accessed 21 March 2023).
27 Tearfund Australia, *They Shall Inherit the Earth: 2022 Tearfund Climate Report* (Blackburn Victoria: Tearfund Australia, 2022), p. 20: tearfund.link/crf (accessed 21 March 2023).
28 Tearfund Australia, *They Shall Inherit the Earth*, p. 20.
29 Farron, *Mucky Business*.
30 Grace Capital City: https://www.gracecapitalcity.com (accessed 27 December 2024).
31 Hayhoe (interview).

32 'Creation Care' at Grace Capital City church: https://www.gracecapitalcity.com/creationcare (accessed 27 December 2024).
33 For medical help, seek out a doctor or psychologist, or contact a mental health helpline in your context.
34 Save the Children, 'Survey Reveals Scale of Climate Anxiety among British Children on Eve of Cop27', 4 November 222: https://www.savethechildren.org.uk/news/media-centre/press-releases/survey-reveals-scale-of-climate-anxiety-among-british-children (accessed 30 July 2024).
35 S. Clayton, C. M. Manning, K. Krygsman and M. Speiser, *Mental Health and Our Changing Climate: Impacts, implications, and guidance* (Washington, D.C.: American Psychological Association, and ecoAmerica, 2017), p. 27: https://www.apa.org/news/press/releases/2017/03/mental-health-climate.pdf (accessed 21 March 2024).
36 Australian Psychological Association, 'Coping with Climate Change Distress': https://psychology.org.au/for-the-public/psychology-topics/climate-change-psychology/coping-with-climate-change-distress (accessed 30 July 2024).
37 UN Environment Programme, '10 Ways You Can Help Fight the Climate Crisis': https://www.unep.org/news-and-stories/story/10-ways-you-can-help-fight-climate-crisis (accessed 21 March 2024).
38 K. Hayhoe, *Saving Us: A climate scientist's case for hope and healing in a divided world* (New York: Simon & Schuster, 2021).
39 Hayhoe (interview).
40 Hayhoe (interview).
41 Hayhoe (interview).
42 H. Malcolm (ed.), *Words for a Dying World: Stories of grief and courage from the global church* (London: SCM, 2020).
43 H.-A. Peterson, 'Faithful, Not Successful', in Malcolm, *Words for a Dying World*, pp. 188–9.
44 T. H. Warren, *Prayer in the Night: For those who work or watch or weep* (Downers Grove: IVP, 2021).
45 Malcolm, *Words for a Dying World*, p. xxxi.
46 A Rocha UK, 'Climate Anxiety and the Church': https://arocha.org.uk/climate-anxiety-and-the-Church/ (accessed 21 March 2024).

47 24-7 Prayer, Tearfund and Renew Our World, 'How to Pray for Climate Change' and 'Pray for the Climate': https://www.renewourworld.net/resources (accessed 21 March 2024).

48 Christian Climate Action: https://christianclimateaction.org/resources/climate-grief-and-anxiety/ (accessed 21 March 2024).

49 D. Bookless and Renew Our World, *Making a World of Difference* (2023), p. 18: https://www.renewourworld.net/resources (accessed 1 January 2024).

50 Stott, *The Birds Our Teachers*, p. 16.

51 Stott, *The Birds Our Teachers*, p. 14.

52 Bookless and Renew Our World, *Making a World of Difference*, pp. 18–19.

53 See M. Ganz, *Why David Sometimes Wins: Leadership, organization, and strategy in the California farm worker movement* (Oxford: Oxford University Press, 2009).

4. Response: listening to global perspectives

1 Anglican Overseas Aid: https://anglicanoverseasaid.org.au/, in partnership with the Anglican Church of Kenya, Diocese of Mount Kenya West.

2 Felistar (interviewee, surname withheld), in person and recorded; interview conducted by J. Knight with an interpreter, 10 March 2023.

3 Bhagwan (interview).

4 Bhagwan (interview).

5 Ray's work in reconciliation has been recognised by the Archbishop of Canterbury: 'Archbishop Presents Pastor Ray Minniecon with Lambeth Award', 11 October 2022: https://www.archbishopofcanterbury.org/priorities/archbishops-commission-families-and-households/news/archbishop-presents-pastor-ray (accessed 21 March 2024).

6 Australians Together, 'The Stolen Generations: The forcible removal of First Nations children from their families': https://australianstogether.org.au/discover-and-learn/our-history/stolen-generations/ (accessed 21 March 2024).

7 Minniecon (interview).
8 In Bookless and Renew Our World, *Making a World of Difference*, p. 29.
9 Minniecon (interview).
10 Minniecon (interview).
11 Minniecon (interview).
12 Australian Geographic, 'DNA Confirms Aboriginal Culture One of Earth's Oldest', 23 September 2011: https://www.australiangeographic.com.au/news/2011/09/dna-confirms-aboriginal-culture-one-of-earths-oldest/ (accessed 5 June 2024).
13 Bringing Them Home, 'Historical Context – Ancient History', Australian Human Rights Commission: https://bth.humanrights.gov.au/significance/historical-context-ancient-history (accessed 5 June 2024).
14 Minniecon (interview).
15 Minniecon (interview).
16 Minniecon (interview).
17 Bhagwan (interview).
18 Bhagwan (interview).
19 Bhagwan (interview).
20 See also, for example, NAIITS (formerly the North American Institute for Indigenous Theological Studies): https://naiits.com/about/ (accessed 6 June 2024).
21 See L. Newbigin, *Foolishness to the Greeks: Gospel and Western culture* (London: SPCK, 1986).
22 D. Bookless, J. Kwong, S. Appiah-Kubi and J. Solano, 'Creation Care', Lausanne Movement: https://lausanne.org/report/sustainable/creation-care (accessed 6 June 2024); and J. Solano, 'The Commodification of the Sacred: A reflection from COP28': https://www.allcreation.org/home/commodification (accessed 6 June 2024).
23 Bookless and Renew Our World, *Making a World of Difference*, p. 30.
24 See Berry and Meitzner Yoder, *John Stott*.
25 The Lord's Prayer drawn from Matthew 6:9–15 as used in the Church of England.

5. Call: tuning into our own calling

1 P. Greig, 'Sabbath Blessing': https://www.dirtyglory.org/new-page-3 (accessed 21 March 2023).
2 T. Rinaudo, *The Forest Underground: Hope for a planet in crisis* (Melbourne: ISCAST, 2022) (Right Livelihood Laureate 2018); and V. Schlöndorff (director), *The Forest Maker* (also known as Ormanların Kurtarıcısı), documentary (zero one film with Volksfilm, 2021): https://www.zeroone.de/en/movies/forestmaker/ (accessed 8 August 2024).
3 Rinaudo (interview).
4 T. Edwards, 'What Happens at 1.5, 2 and 4°C of Global Warming?', in Thunberg, *Climate Book*, p. 125.
5 R. Valerio, *Saying Yes to Life: The Archbishop of Canterbury's Lent book 2020* (London: SPCK, 2019).
6 R. Valerio, *L Is for Lifestyle: Christian living that doesn't cost the earth* (rev. edn; London: IVP, 2019). For a full list of publications, see https://ruthvalerio.net/ (accessed 26 August 2025).
7 C. Seaton, *Whose Earth?* (Cambridge: Crossway, 1992).
8 Valerio (interview).
9 Valerio (interview).
10 Rokhum (interview).
11 Rokhum (interview).
12 Rokhum (interview).
13 Rokhum (interview).
14 UN Sustainable Development Goals, 'Be the Change': https://www.un.org/sustainabledevelopment/be-the-change (accessed 22 August 2024).
15 Rokhum (interview).
16 Rinaudo (interview).
17 Bookless (interview).
18 Bookless (interview).
19 D. Bookless, *God Doesn't Do Waste: Redeeming the whole of life* (Nottingham: IVP, 2010).
20 R. P. DeBorst, 'Intertwining Roots for Just Conviviality', in Meitzner Yoder, *Living Radical Discipleship*, p. 72.

21 A. de Mello, *Sadhana: A Way to God; Christian exercises in Eastern form* (Melbourne: Harper Collins, 1998), p. 126.
22 de Mello, *Sadhana*, p. 126.

6. Response: being part of something bigger

1 Hayhoe (interview).
2 The United Nations reports of the Intergovernmental Panel on Climate Change (IPCC) urge responsible, immediate and urgent reduction as actions to help manage the crisis.
3 See Project Drawdown: https://drawdown.org/ (accessed 1 August 2024).
4 Bhagwan (interview).
5 E. Endara, 'Every Action Matters: A Q&A with climate scientist, Katharine Hayhoe', 23 November 2021, Oxfam America: https://www.oxfamamerica.org/explore/stories/every-action-matters-a-qa-with-climate-scientist-katharine-hayhoe/ (accessed 21 March 2024).
6 Hayhoe, *Saving Us*, p. 185; and E. Pattee, 'Leading Climate Scientist Katharine Hayhoe: "You have the ability to use your voice"', *The Guardian*, 10 November 2021: https://www.theguardian.com/environment/2021/nov/10/katharine-hayoe-climate-change-interview (accessed 21 March 2024).
7 E. Chenowith, 'People Power', in Thunberg, *Climate Book*, p. 368.
8 See R. Gower and R. Walker, *The Hopeful Activist: Discovering the vital change you were made to bring* (London: SPCK, 2024), ch. 6; and Tearfund, 'Advocacy Toolkit – A Roots guide': https://learn.tearfund.org/en/resources/series/roots-guides/advocacy-toolkit--a-roots-guide (accessed 30 July 2024).
9 Hayhoe (interview).
10 Bookless (interview).

Conclusion

1 Ephesians 3:20–21.